D0469747

Eric Oakley Parrott was born in 19... within the sound of Bow Bells, and so was te........ ....y, but was brought up in Shoreham-by-Sea, Sussex, where he attended the local grammar school. After winning that school's most coveted academic award, the Gregory Taylor Scholarship, in 1939, he went to Brighton Technical College, where he studied for a BSc in Mathematics and Geography. He then spent twenty years as a cartographer with the Hydrographic Department of the Ministry of Defence, and while there edited the Admiralty List of Radio Signals. He began to write seriously in his spare time – articles, plays and entries in various literary competitions. He always took a keen interest in the theatre and was both an amateur actor and a producer, becoming an Associate of the Drama Board in 1961. He had a number of his plays produced and his radio plays have been performed by the BBC and in Germany, Canada, Australia and New Zealand, among other countries. In 1976 he resigned from the Civil Service, and, after a year at Garnet College, Roehampton, taught English and general studies at Havering Technical College, Hornchurch, Essex. Here he compiled a number of Units for the Longman's General Studies Project. Failing eyesight forced him to retire from teaching and he then began a third career as a full-time writer. His books include *Limerick Delight* (Puffin), *Imitations of Immortality*, *How to Become Ridiculously Well-Read in One Evening*, *How to Become Absurdly Well-Informed About the Famous and the Infamous*, *How to Be Well-Versed in Poetry*, *The Dogsbody Papers* and *How to Be Tremendously Tuned In to Opera*, all published by Penguin.

Eric Oakley Parrott died in November 1990.

27. 7. 92

Dear Mrs Kagerer,

We thank you very much for your help + interest in our works.

your English Department

(R. Stingl-Sch.)

The Penguin Book of

COMPILED AND EDITED BY
E. O. PARROTT

ILLUSTRATIONS BY ROBIN JACQUES

PENGUIN BOOKS

To my darling Tricia
Without whom the road to Limerick
would have ended prematurely in
the Slough of Despond.

PENGUIN BOOKS

Published by the Penguin Group
Penguin Books Ltd, 27 Wrights Lane, London W8 5TZ, England
Penguin Books USA Inc., 375 Hudson Street, New York, New York 10014, USA
Penguin Books Australia Ltd, Ringwood, Victoria, Australia
Penguin Books Canada Ltd, 10 Alcorn Avenue, Toronto, Ontario, Canada M4V 3B2
Penguin Books (NZ) Ltd, 182–190 Wairau Road, Auckland 10, New Zealand

Penguin Books Ltd, Registered Offices: Harmondsworth, Middlesex, England

First published in Great Britain by Allen Lane 1983
First published in the United States of America by Viking 1986
Published in Penguin Books 1984
9 10 8

Photoset in Linnotron 202 Bembo by Wyvern Typesetting Ltd, Bristol
Printed in Great Britain by
BPCC Hazell Books
Aylesbury, Bucks, England
Member of BPCC Ltd.

CONTENTS

INTRODUCTION

Here is a collection of some eight hundred limericks, together with a modest selection of material from what may be termed the 'Limerick Fringe'. But are they all 'good' limericks? And anyway, what is the justification for so large an anthology devoted to this simple verse form? One answer to the latter question would seem to be that the limerick arouses such strong feelings in its devotees. There are passionate views about what a limerick should or should not be, and what it ought or ought not to be about. No other verse form seems to give rise to such strong feelings of loyalty. The United States (where else?) even boasts at least two societies devoted to it.

In a letter written to me soon after I began work on this collection, Dr Robert Conquest said that another distinguished English publishing house had abandoned a similar project some years ago on the grounds that there were no more than a couple of hundred verses worthy of inclusion. This did not look any too promising. Other authorities sounded equally pessimistic. Jean Harrowven, in the introduction to her useful and scholarly history of the limerick, *The Limerick Makers* (Research Publishing Co., 1976), put forward some very definite views on the subject of limerick anthologies: 'A straight collection of limericks would be boring. The restricted pattern of the metre would lend itself to monotony.' Having read through some ten thousand limericks in the course of my labours, this is a view with which I can sympathize, but which I reject. For if there is one thing that has impressed me, it is the astonishing variety of the material written in this simple verse form. There is sophisticated wit and bawdy humour, satire and barbed social comment, nonsense and fantasy, wry irony and, yes, even quite serious limericks. The spectrum is too broad for there to be any danger of boredom – to my mind anyway. Mrs Harrowven's fears seem to presuppose that readers would be foolish enough to read a limerick anthology straight through from cover to cover. My aim was to produce a book that can be browsed through, or dipped into from time to time.

My reading soon convinced me that Dr Conquest's doubts were misplaced, too – there were more than enough good limericks for my purpose, although it depended, as Dr C. E. M. Joad might have said, on what one meant by a 'good limerick'. There is a considerable body of authoritative opinion which avers that a limerick is an indecent verse or it is nothing – well, nothing worth reading anyway. The two classic modern collections of indecent limericks are both by Gershon Legman (*The Limerick*, Jupiter Books, 1974, and *The New Limerick Book*, Crown Publishing, 1979). A limerick from the second of these volumes perhaps summarizes this view:

> The limerick form is so easy,
> It's no trick at all to be breezy;
>   But the lines of its wit
>   Are oft flavoured with shit,
> Arousing the qualms of the queasy.

When collecting material for this book, I found that the response to my question 'Do you know any good limericks?' was often 'Yes, but none that you would put into your book'. I find this a rather old-fashioned attitude in view of our current permissiveness. On the other hand, I would have thought that most people were capable of appreciating wit and humour based upon the whole gamut of human activities. Jokes, to be good, do not *have* to be about sex.

The opposite view was put succinctly by Dr Cyril Bibby in his comprehensive study of the verse form, *The Art of the Limerick* (Research Publishing Co., 1978): 'No consideration, not even a deep commitment to the objectivity of research, could persuade me to give many of these verses wider circulation.' As he neatly puts it:

> The limerick verse has its attraction,
> The ribald may give satisfaction,
>   But I never have fancied,
>   The nastily rancid
> Or verses of sick putrefaction.

W. S. Baring-Gould, in his admirably catholic collection, *The Lure of the Limerick* (Rupert Hart-Davis, 1968), argues against the publishing of verses with certain 'words' in them; this, too, I feel is now an outdated attitude.

I propose to defer, for the moment, any further discussion regarding the criteria which I have employed in the selection of material for this anthology, since, before doing so, I feel it would be useful to take a brief, unscholarly look at the history and development of the limerick. Indeed certain aspects of the arrangement of this collection cannot be fully understood without that information.

Contrary to popular belief, Edward Lear did not invent the limerick. Although he may have played some part in popularizing it, there is ample evidence to suggest that it was widely known by the time he published his first *Book of Nonsense* in 1846. He himself puts it quite clearly in his introduction to the second, expanded edition of his original work, *The Book of Nonsense and More Nonsense* (1862):

> Long years ago, in days when much of my time was passed in a country house, where children and mirth abounded, the lines beginning 'There was an old man of Tobago' were suggested to me by a valued friend as a form of verse lending itself to limitless variety for rhymes and pictures; and thenceforth the greater part of the original drawings and verses for the first 'Book of Nonsense' were struck off with a pen, no assistance ever having been given me in any way but that of uproarious delight and welcome at the appearance of every new absurdity.

The reference to 'assistance' reveals that Lear was concerned to deny rumours which had been circulating since the publication of the first *Book of Nonsense* that it was the work of, among others, the deceased Earl of Derby, for whose children the rhymes had been written between 1836 and 1839, when Lear had been employed by the Earl as a botanical illustrator. It was in fact in this artistic field, and not as the author of nonsense verses, that Lear had hoped to be successful, as Langford Reed's limerick on page 25 of this book makes clear.

Limerick-type verses were quite well known long before Lear published his first collection. As Dr Cyril Bibby has pointed out in *The Art of the Limerick*, in December 1845 *Punch* was commenting: '. . . Our old friends the Old Man of Tobago, the Sailor of Bister, etc. have been excluded from the Most Gracious Schoolroom for an entirely new class of picture books. . .' 'The Old Man of Tobago' was one of the eponymous heroes of *Anecdotes and Adventures of Fifteen Gentlemen*, published in 1822. The author is not known with any degree of certainty. It had been preceded two years earlier by a similar book of rhymes, *The History of Sixteen Wonderful Old Women*. Dr Bibby shows conclusively that Lear not only knew this second book but that he borrowed the idea for his illustration for *The Owl and the Pussycat* from the picture that had accompanied one of the rhymes about these Wonderful Old Women:

> There was an Old Woman called Towl
> Who went to sea with an Owl;
> > But the Owl was sea-sick,
> > And screamed for physic,
> Which sadly annoyed Mistress Towl.

We would recognize all the rhymes in both books as what we now call 'limericks'. No one has been able to discover any verses earlier than these which would qualify for the name. Poets had been using the 'limerick' metre and rhyming scheme for hundreds of years. Thomas Moore, the Irish poet (1779–1852), for example:

> The time I've lost in wooing,
> In watching and pursuing,
> > The light that lies
> > In women's eyes
> Has been my heart's undoing.

There are many other examples of verses with a strong family likeness to the limerick, from the chorus to Stephano's song in Shakespeare's *The Tempest* to this, from an eleventh-century manuscript:

> The lion is wondrous strong
> And full of the wiles of wo;
> > And whether he pleye
> > Or take his preye,
> He cannot do but slo [slay].

There are scholars who think *Summer is icumen in* is a precursor of the limerick, and others who have found similarities between the choruses in Greek comedies of 400 BC and the limerick, but such speculations would seem to me to be of academic interest only; the fact remains that Mistress Towl and the Old Man of Tobago are the only early verses that we can with any degree of certainty call 'limericks'.

Jean Harrowven in *The Limerick Makers* does some special pleading for a group of Irish poets who were active in the middle of the eighteenth century, and whom she cheerily designates 'the merry poets of Croom'. Certainly the verses they wrote in their drinking sessions at the public house run by one of their number, John O'Tuomy, were in the limerick form, but they were of course in Irish and no English translation was available until 1840, by which time the Old Man of Tobago and friends had already been going the rounds for twenty years. Nor is there much similarity between the tavern verses of the Croom poets and the limericks fathered by the Old Man of Tobago:

> I sell the best brandy and sherry
> To make my good customers merry,
> But at times their finances
> Run short as it chances,
> And then I feel very sad, very.

Their importance as far as the modern limerick is concerned seems to lie in furnishing a probable explanation as to how the verse came to be known as the limerick. It is not unreasonable to surmise that the tavern songs of the Croom poets and their imitators crossed the Irish Sea in the eighteenth and nineteenth centuries with the immigrant labourers who came to work as navvies, factory hands and so forth. Bawdy parodies of Lear's limericks by Swinburne and others were soon circulating in England (from the 1860s onwards), and it seems likely that sooner or later both lots of verses, which were by an historical accident prosodically identical, became known by the name that had already been given to the verses fathered by the Croom poets. *The Oxford Dictionary*, incidentally, gives 1892 as the date of the first use of the word 'limerick' – four years after Lear's death.

Another parodist of Lear's Nonsense limericks was W. S. Gilbert, whose limerick about the Old Man of St Bee's, the first unrhymed limerick, is given in the historical section of this book ('Genesis', page 29). The form clearly had its attractions for Gilbert, who used it in many of his lyrics and poems, as for example:

> Oh, my name is John Wellington Wells,
> I'm a dealer in magic and spells,
> Of blessings and curses,
> And ever-filled purses,
> In prophecies, witches and knells.

(THE SORCERER)

11

A man who would woo a fair maid,
He should 'prentice himself to the trade,
    And study all day
    In methodical way
How to flatter, cajole and persuade.

(THE YEOMEN OF THE GUARD)

By the end of the nineteenth century, both branches of limerick writing – the clean and the indecent – were flourishing. Their composition was considered a pleasant literary exercise by men of letters, both professional and amateur, who found the form particularly apt for a wide variety of humorous verses. Clean ones were widely published, whilst indecent ones were printed privately or circulated orally. Notable limerick-writers included Dante Gabriel Rossetti, Lord Tennyson, Mark Twain and many, many others. Clean limericks published in *Punch* and other magazines often depended on weak puns or the curiosities of English pronunciation:

There was a young chappie called Cholmondley,
Who always at dinner sat dolmondley;
    His fair partner said
    As he crumbled his bread:
'Dear me, you do behave romondley.'

In the first decade of the twentieth century, limerick writing received an enormous boost in popularity when a number of newspapers ran weekly competitions, which usually involved supplying the final line for some given verse. Enormous prizes were on offer, such as furnished houses, an income for life, etc., and the sale of sixpenny postal orders – the usual entry fee – soared to fantastic heights. Newspapers and advertising companies still use limerick competitions, but there is nothing like the nationwide interest of those early days. The limerick also became a favourite vehicle for satirizing public figures. This is from *Punch* in 1918:

There was a young man of Moose Jaw,
Who wanted to see Bernard Shaw;
    When they questioned him why,
    He made no reply,
But sharpened his circular saw.

In the United States in 1902 Carolyn Wells published the first of her several anthologies of anonymous and other clean limericks, to which she added many of her own. Unfortunately, much of the humour has dated or seems rather limp by modern standards, but one can see how funny they must have been at the time:

> There once was a discreet Brigadier,
> Very fond of Four Thousand a Year,
>   Who, when he heard the guns rattle,
>   Fiercely cried: 'Ha! The battle!'
> Then complacently slid to the rear.

In Britain in 1924 Langford Reed, a journalist, published *The Complete Limerick Book*, an anthology of clean limericks. Many were anonymous, but some were by known authors, including himself. It is surprising how many of these innocent verses have survived and are still anthologized today – there are a number in this book. However, many seem very weak, and I doubt if they were terribly funny even at that time.

> There was a young angler of Worthing,
> Who dug up ten worms and a fur thing;
>   He said: 'How I wish
>   Eleven fine fish
> Would snap up these things I'm unearthing.'

Such examples make me sympathize with Gershon Legman's sharp condemnation of the clean limerick, although I think his strictures go too far:

The limerick is, and was originally, an indecent verse form. The clean sort of limerick is an obvious palliation [sic]; its content insipid, its rhyming artificially ingenious, its whole permeated and pervaded with a frustrated nonsense that vents itself typically in explosive and aggressive violence. There are, certainly, aggressive bawdy limericks too, but they are not in the majority. Except as the maidenly delight and silly delectation of a few elderly gentlemen, such as the late Langford Reed, and several still living, who might as well remain nameless, the clean limerick has never been of the slightest interest to anyone.

Leaving aside the initial generalization, which is of dubious historical accuracy, it seems to me that the trouble with many of the clean limericks is that they are downright unaggressive, weak and often boring to our modern taste. On the other hand, much the same criticism can be made of very many of the indecent limericks where the mere mention of sexual perversion, the loss of virginity, strange ways with excrement, and so forth, is meant to give rise to hilarity. In many, the 'joke' is clearly the use of some of those long-unpublished 'words' for sexual organs and activities; they are mere lavatory humour, and, as in the case of graffiti, wit is confined to a small proportion of the total output.

There has always been a traffic between the clean and indecent limerick streams. Laundered versions of indecent verses were quite common, and many a clean limerick has been adapted to transform it into an indecent one. This may not make it any funnier. Thus, the limerick about the gourmet of Crewe who complained about a dead mouse in his stew becomes, in the indecent version:

> There was a young lady of Crewe
> Found an elephant's whang in her stew.

The remainder of the limerick remains unaltered.

The indecent limerick has traditionally been a joke for men, a verse to be recited in smoke-filled bars or clubhouses, at business-men's conferences or in rugger changing-rooms. Its humour is often of the blackest. We are asked to laugh at rape, necrophilia, bestiality and buggery. A great deal of it may be seen as the humour of the Male Chauvinist Pig. How much amusement this affords the reader will depend upon individual taste and what is acceptable in society at the time. There are anti-Jewish limericks, anti-Irish limericks and, indeed, every kind of racist limerick. All humour is to a greater or lesser extent cruel and any judgement as to what is or is not acceptable must be subjective, so here I have followed my own feelings. Having read several thousands of these indecent limericks, I can understand Dr Bibby's condemnation of many of them as 'repulsive'. Gershon Legman, in his introduction to *The New Limerick Book*, makes it clear that he feels the same way about much of the material he has collected over the years. His books are of interest not because we find all the limericks funny, but because of what they tell us about a society which has laughed at them over the years.

Because of their subject matter and language, most indecent limericks are anonymous. There are notable exceptions, however, such as those by Norman Douglas. More recently Isaac Asimov has published a number of volumes of what he calls 'Lecherous Limericks', and I was grateful to Mrs Catley of New Zealand for sending me a volume of her late husband's limericks which is very much in the 'indecent limerick' tradition. In the last fifty years or so, it has become common for the cleaner limericks to be published under their authors' names. Thomas Thorneley, Anthony Euwer, Professor Morris Bishop, E. V. Knox, Ogden Nash and others have either published volumes of limericks or included them in their collections of verse. Edward Gorey gave the limerick a new dimension of Gothic horror. Gavin Ewart and W. H. Auden both include limericks in their volumes of poetry, and Walter de la Mare has a number of double limericks in the collected edition of his work.

A third group of limericks can now be distinguished, which one might call the 'intellectual stream'. One of the most famous is by Ronald Knox about Bishop Berkeley's theory of the nature of reality, to which there was an anonymous riposte. Many other verses upon such subjects as philosophy, science, art and literature followed from a variety of authors, both known and unknown. In the 1930s there were notable literary competitions in the *New Statesman and Nation* and the *Spectator*. Both included a considerable number of limerick competitions, and from the first they attracted entries from a large number of distinguished and talented writers, professional and amateur. At various times since, similar regular competitions were run in the *Church Times*, *Punch*, *Time and Tide* and *John O'London's Weekly*. All included limerick competitions from time to time, and the *Spectator* at one stage ran one every week. Many of the limericks are very dated, but one does not need to have read the original essay by Rose Macaulay to appreciate this verse by Rose Vines from an early *Spectator* competition:

> That essay by Miss Rose Macaulay
> Has made me go all creepy-crawly;
> My brain feels torpescent
> Those words so turgescent
> Are not all in the dictionary, surely?

Inevitably, the competition limericks remained in the 'clean' or 'intellectual' limerick tradition until the relaxation of censorship controls from the 1960s onwards. The subjects are remarkably varied – philosophy, science, disease, fish, the Devil, celebrations of

Bernard Shaw's ninetieth birthday, contemporary figures, French towns, fictional persons and places, and many other topics. There are potted versions of famous poems, novels or plays, and comments on famous paintings. Occasionally the jokes induce a smile rather than a laugh, as in this typical example by 'Little Billee' from the *New Statesman* of September 1945:

> There once was a naughty old salmon,
> Who maintained that he served God and Mammon,
>   But please understand
>   The poor fish was canned
> When he talked this nonsensical gammon.

Many professional writers found the weekly competitions a challenge to their ingenuity and literary skill. ('Write one sentence of perfect English prose,' *Time and Tide* asked one week.) Names such as John Betjeman, Walter de la Mare, Frances Cornford, Bernard Levin and Terence Rattigan crop up among the entrants, and it is certain that many of the pseudonyms employed hide other well-known contributors, although it is probably no longer possible to identify them. The competitions also attracted a group of enthusiasts who, over the years, became remarkably adept at producing highly skilled entries in verse and prose on almost any subject and in almost any form or style.

I trust that, by now, my criteria for the selection of material for this book will have become apparent. I wanted the limericks to be good, with some real point that still makes its effect today. They had also to be technically faultless, with no false rhymes. However amusing, I could find no place for limericks such as this:

> A widow who lived in Rangoon
> Hung a rather large wreath on her womb;
>   'It reminds me,' she said,
>   'Of my husband who's dead,
> And how he got into his tomb.'

I did not demand that all limericks should provide belly laughs; indeed, subtlety and gentle wry humour were to be duly represented, and I also included a number of serious or semi-serious limericks, since my aim was to show the whole extent of the limerick world. Nevertheless, where a joke was intended it had to be a good one. A little regretfully, therefore, I excluded a number of familiar limericks where the humour seems to be rather too crudely schoolboyish. Thus departed the Old Man of Blackheath who sat on his set of false teeth, and who announced to the world that he had bitten himself underneath. With him and his many fellows went some, like this one, where there is no real joke other than the spelling of the words to accord with that at the end of the first line:

> A lady who lived by the Thames
> Had a gorgeous collection of ghames;
>   She had them re-set
>   In a large coronet
> And a number of small diadhames.

Even where limericks seemed good and amusing at first sight, they often turned out to be using the same joke as another verse. Thus the limerick about a young man called Cyril and his amorous relationship with a squirrel was too reminiscent of Myrtle and her affair with a turtle. It was Cyril who had to go. Neither could I find much to enjoy in the hard porn end of the collections of indecent limericks. There had to be enough humour or wit to redeem the subject; crude bawdiness, reminding me of poor seaside postcards of days gone by, seldom seemed to be enough:

> There was a young man of Bulgaria,
> Who went for a piss in an area;
>   Said Mary to cook:
>   'Oh, do come and look.
> Did you ever see anything hairier?'

Throughout the book, I have been concerned to choose the best limericks in each of the many categories, arranging them in such a way as to reveal the wide-ranging variety of style and subject that finds expression in this simple verse form.

Like another book (which, I believe, sells rather well), I begin with 'Genesis' and end with 'Revelations'. The former is intended to give the collection some historical perspective, whilst the latter deliberately aims at those who like an uninterrupted read of the bawdier sort of limerick. Elsewhere the material has been somewhat arbitrarily arranged according to subject. One section, 'Airs Grave and Gentle', is devoted to the rather more serious and wryly humorous verses. In 'The Limerick Fringe' I have given as many examples as space permitted of the various verse forms which the limerick has fathered – the double limerick, the limick, the extended limerick, the unrhymed limerick, and so on. There are a few groups of more specialized forms of the verse – tongue-twisters and beheaded limericks – while three small sections are devoted to limericks which have been written within very strict limits: in two, the first line was already (more or less) determined, while the third gives variations on the well-known limerick about 'the family Stein'. One of the limericks in these groups, although awarded a prize in the *New Statesman*, was not printed in the magazine on the grounds that it was too indecent!

I have recorded elsewhere my thanks to all those who sent me verses, either their own work or those they had come across. I was glad to find that there are still plenty of people writing limericks for their own and other people's pleasure. I was particularly gratified by the response of one clergyman who wrote to say that he had never written a limerick before, but on seeing my appeal in the *Church Times* had sat down and written me some. It would be pleasant to think that this book may provoke a similar response from all its readers. After all, most limerick writing has been done for enjoyment; although many have earned money by publishing limericks, I doubt if anyone has ever earned a living from them. It has been the literary pursuit of the amateur.

Those who are addicted to literary competitions know the pleasure that is to be got from a few hours a week devoted to writing creatively. The writing of diaries, letters and poetry for their own sake and with no eye to publication seems to be on the decline, and yet there is no finer way of educating ourselves to appreciate any craft than by trying to practise it. So, come on now. There is plenty of room in the ranks of 'Anon.'

E. O. PARROTT

Prologue

Our existence would be that much grimmer except for the solace of limericks.
   – A fact that's unknown
   To two lots alone
– The drearier dons and the dimmer hicks.

ROBERT CONQUEST

Self-Portraits

The limerick is furtive and mean;
You must keep her in close quarantine,
    Or she sneaks to the slums
    And promptly becomes
Disorderly, drunk and obscene.

MORRIS BISHOP

It needn't have ribaldry's taint
Or strive to make everyone faint.
    There's a type that's demure
    And perfectly pure,
Though it helps quite a lot if it ain't.

DON MARQUIS

The limerick packs laughs anatomical
Into space that is quite economical,
    But the good ones I've seen
    So seldom are clean,
And the clean ones so seldom are comical.

ANON.

A bather whose clothing was strewed
By winds, that left her quite nude,
    Saw a man come along,
    And, unless I am wrong,
You expected this line to be rude.

ANON.

The limerick's callous and crude,
Its morals distressingly lewd;
    It's not worth the reading
    By persons of breeding –
It's designed for us vulgar and rude.

ANON.

At Harvard a randy old Dean
Said: 'The funniest jokes are obscene.
    To bowdlerize wit
    Takes the shit out of it –
Who wants a limerick clean?'

ANON.

There was a young lady . . . tut, tut!
So you think that you're in for some smut?
    Some five-line crescendo
    Of lewd innuendo?
Well, you're wrong. This is anything but.

STANLEY J. SHARPLESS

I'm bored to extinction with Harrison,
His limericks and puns are embarrassin'.
    But I'm fond of the bum,
    For, though dull as they come,
He makes me feel bright by comparison.

ANON.

Genesis

The limerick's birth is unclear;
Its GENESIS owed much to Lear.
   It started as clean,
   But soon went obscene,
And this split haunts its later career.

There was an Old Woman of Lynn,
Whose Nose very near reach'd her chin;
   You may easy suppose
   She had plenty of Beaux,
This charming Old Woman of Lynn.

The History of Sixteen Wonderful Old Women (1820).
Author unknown

There was an Old Woman of Gloster,
Whose parrot two guineas it cost her;
   But his tongue never ceasing,
   Was vastly displeasing,
To that talkative Woman of Gloster.

The History of Sixteen Wonderful Old Women (1820).
Author unknown

There was a sick man of Tobago,
Lived long on rice-gruel and sago;
   But at last to his bliss,
   The physician said this:
'To a roast leg of mutton you may go.'

Anecdotes and Adventures of Fifteen Gentlemen (1822).
Author unknown

There was an Old Miser of Reading,
Had a house, with a yard, with a shed in;
   'Twas meant for a cow,
   But so small that I vow
The poor creature could scarce get its head in.

Anecdotes and Adventures of Fifteen Gentlemen (1822).
Author unknown

[*Upon Edward Lear*]

A goddess capricious is Fame,
You may try to make noted your name,
   But she either rejects you,
   Or coolly selects you
For laurels distinct from your aim.

LANGFORD REED
(1889–1954)

There was a Young Lady whose chin
Resembled the point of a pin;
   So she had it made sharp,
   And purchased a harp,
And played several tunes with her chin.

EDWARD LEAR
(1812–1888)

There was an Old Person of Hurst,
Who drank when he was a-thirst;
   When they said: 'You'll grow fatter!'
   He answered: 'No matter!'
That globular Old Person of Hurst.

EDWARD LEAR

There was an Old Man who supposed
That the street door was partially closed;
   But some very large rats
   Ate his coats and his hats
While that futile Old Gentleman dozed.

EDWARD LEAR

There was an Old Man who said: 'Hush!
I perceive a young bird in this bush!'
   When they said: 'Is it small?'
   He replied: 'Not at all!
It is four times as big as the bush.'

EDWARD LEAR

There was an Old Man of Thermopylae,
Who never did anything properly;
   But they said: 'If you choose
   To boil eggs in your shoes,
You shall never remain in Thermopylae.'

EDWARD LEAR

There was an Old Person of Cromer,
Who stood on one leg to read Homer;
   When he found he grew stiff,
   He jumped over the cliff,
Which concluded that Person of Cromer.

EDWARD LEAR

There was an Old Man who said: 'How
Shall I flee from that horrible cow?
   I will sit on this stile,
   And continue to smile,
Which may soften the heart of that cow.'

EDWARD LEAR

There was an Old Man of the coast,
Who placidly sat on a post;
   But when it was cold,
   He relinquished his hold,
And called for some hot buttered toast.
EDWARD LEAR

There was an Old Man who said: 'Well!
Will *nobody* answer that bell?
   I have pulled day and night,
   Till my hair has turned white,
But nobody answers this bell.'
EDWARD LEAR

There was a Young Girl of Majorca,
Whose aunt was a very fast walker;
   She walked seventy miles,
   And leaped fifteen stiles,
Which astounded that Girl of Majorca.
EDWARD LEAR

There was an Old Man on whose nose
Most birds of the air would repose;
   But they all flew away
   At the closing of day,
Which relieved that Old Man and his nose.
EDWARD LEAR

There was an Old Man of Cape Horn,
Who wished he had never been born:
   So he sat on a chair,
   Till he died of despair,
That dolorous Man of Cape Horn.

EDWARD LEAR

There was a young man of Cape Horn,
Who wished he had never been born,
   Nor would he have been
   If his father had seen
That the end of the rubber was torn.

ALGERNON CHARLES SWINBURNE(?)
(1837–1909)

There was a Young Lady of Ryde
Whose shoelaces were seldom untied;
   She purchased some clogs
   And some small spotted dogs,
And frequently walked about Ryde.

EDWARD LEAR

There was a fat lady of Clyde,
Whose shoelaces once came untied;
   She didn't dare stoop,
   For fear she would poop,
So she cried and she cried and she cried.

ANON.

There was a Young Lady of Norway,
Who casually sat in a doorway;
   When the door squeezed her flat,
   She exclaimed: 'What of that?'
This courageous Young Lady of Norway.
                    EDWARD LEAR

There was a young lady of Norway,
Who hung by her toes in a doorway;
   She said to her beau:
   'Come over here, Joe,
I think I've discovered one more way!'
     ALGERNON CHARLES SWINBURNE (?)

There was an Old Man in a tree,
Who was horribly stung by a bee;
   When they said: 'Does it buzz?'
   He replied: 'Yes, it does.
It's a regular brute of a bee!'
                    EDWARD LEAR

There was an old man of St Bees
Who was horribly stung by a wasp.
   When they said: 'Does it hurt?'
   He replied: 'No, it doesn't –
It's a good job it wasn't a hornet!'
         SIR WILLIAM S. GILBERT
              (1836–1911)

There was a young girl of Aberystwyth,
Who took grain to the mill to make grist with.
   The miller's son, Jack,
   Laid her on her back,
And united the organs they pissed with.
ALGERNON CHARLES SWINBURNE (?)

The Reverend Henry Ward Beecher
Called a hen a most elegant creature,
   The hen, pleased with that,
   Laid an egg in his hat,
And thus did the hen reward Beecher.
OLIVER WENDELL HOLMES
(1809–1894)

There is an old he-wolf named Gambart,
Beware of him if thou a lamb art;
   Else thy tail and thy toes,
   And thy innocent nose,
Will be ground by the grinder of Gambart.
DANTE GABRIEL ROSSETTI
(1828–1882)

There is a creature called God,
Whose creations are some of them odd.
   I maintain, and I shall,
   The creation of Val
Reflects little credit on God.
DANTE GABRIEL ROSSETTI

There's a combative artist named Whistler
Who is, like his own hog-hairs, a bristler;
   A tube of white lead,
   And a punch on the head
Offer varied attractions to Whistler.
                       DANTE GABRIEL ROSSETTI

There's a Portuguese person named Howell,
Who lays on his lies with a trowel;
   Should he give over lying,
   T'will be when he's dying,
For living is lying with Howell.
                       DANTE GABRIEL ROSSETTI

There once was a painter named Scott,
Who seemed to have hair, but had not.
   He seemed to have sense,
   'Twas an equal pretence
On the part of the painter named Scott.
                       DANTE GABRIEL ROSSETTI

There's an Irishman, Arthur O'Shaughnessy –
On the chessboard of poets a pawn is he;
   Though a bishop or king
   Would be rather the thing
To the fancy of Arthur O'Shaughnessy.
                       DANTE GABRIEL ROSSETTI

There is a big artist named Val,
The roughs' and the prize-fighters' pal.
   The mind of a groom
   And the head of a broom
Were Nature's endowments to Val.

DANTE GABRIEL ROSSETTI

There's a publishing party named Ellis,
Who's addicted to poets with bellies.
   He has at least two –
   One in fact, one in view –
And God knows what will happen to Ellis.

DANTE GABRIEL ROSSETTI

There is a poor sneak called Rossetti,
As a painter with many kicks met he –
   With more as a man –
   But sometimes he ran,
And that saved the rear of Rossetti.

DANTE GABRIEL ROSSETTI

There was a young lady of station.
'I love man' was her exclamation,
   But when men cried: 'You flatter!'
   She replied: 'Oh, no matter!'
'Isle of Man' is the explanation.

LEWIS CARROLL
(REV. CHARLES LUTWIDGE DODGSON)
(1832–1898)

There was once a young man of Oporto,
Who daily got shorter and shorter;
     The reason he said
     Was the hod on his head,
Which was filled with the heaviest mortar.

LEWIS CARROLL

His sister, called Lucy O'Finner,
Grew constantly thinner and thinner;
     The reason was plain,
     She slept out in the rain,
And was never allowed any dinner.

LEWIS CARROLL

There was a young lady of Whitby,
Who had the bad luck to be bit by
     Two brown little things
     Without any wings,
And now she's uncomfy to sit by.

LEWIS CARROLL

A man hired by John Smith and Co.
Loudly declared that he'd tho.
     Men that he saw
     Dumping dirt near his door –
The drivers, therefore, didn't do.

MARK TWAIN
(SAMUEL LANGHORNE CLEMENS)
(1835–1910)

A spelling reformer indicted
For fudge, was before the court cited.
   The judge said: 'Enough!
   Your candle we'll snough,
His sepulchre shall not be wighted.'

AMBROSE BIERCE
(1842–1914)

There was a young lady of Limerick,
Who stole from a farmer named Tim a rick;
   When the priest at the altar
   Suggested a halter,
She fled from the county of Limerick.

ANDREW LANG
(1844–1912)

There was an old man of the Cape,
Who made himself garments of crepe.
   When asked: 'Do they tear?'
   He replied: 'Here and there,
But they're perfectly splendid for shape.'

ROBERT LOUIS STEVENSON
(1850–1894)

There was a young genius of Queen's,
Who was fond of exploding machines.
   He once blew up a door,
   But he'll do it no more,
For it chanced that the door was the Dean's.

ARTHUR CLEMENT HILTON
(1851–1877)

There was an Old Fellow of Trinity,
A Doctor well versed in Divinity,
But he took to free thinking,
And then to deep drinking,
And so had to leave the vicinity.

ARTHUR CLEMENT HILTON

There was a young critic of King's,
Who had views on the limits of things.
With the size of his chapel,
He would frequently grapple,
And exclaim: 'It is biggish for King's.'

ARTHUR CLEMENT HILTON

There was a young gourmand of John's,
Who'd a notion of dining on swans.
To the Backs he took big nets
To capture the cygnets,
But was told they were kept for the dons.

ARTHUR CLEMENT HILTON

There was a young student of John's,
Who wanted to bugger some swans.
But the loyal hall-porter
Said: 'Please take my daughter,
For the swans are reserved for the Dons.'

ANON.

There was a great German Grammarian,
Whose grandmother wasn't an Aryan,
  So his books have been burned
  And his person interned,
And his doctrine denounced as barbarian.

THOMAS THORNELEY
(1855–1949)

There was an old man of Bengal,
Who purchased a bat and a ball,
  Some gloves and some pads;
  It was one of his fads,
For he never played cricket at all.

F. ANSTEY
(THOMAS ANSTEY GUTHRIE)
(1856–1934)

For hours my wife says 'Goodbye,'
And a marvel of patience am I;
  I can bridle my passion,
  Through servants and fashion,
But at the mention of babies, I fly.

GELETT BURGESS
(1860–1951)

I'd rather have fingers than toes,
I'd rather have ears than a nose;
  As for my hair,
  I'm glad it's still there,
I'll be awfully sad when it goes.

GELETT BURGESS

There was a good Canon of Durham,
Who fished with a hook and a worrum;
   Said the Dean to the Bishop;
    'I've brought a big fish up,
But I fear we may have to inter'm.'

W.R.INGE
(1860–1954)

There was an old man of Khartoum,
Who kept two black sheep in his room.
   'To remind me,' he said,
    'Of some people who're dead,
But I never can recollect whom.'

W.R.INGE

There was a small boy of Quebec,
Who was buried in snow to his neck.
   When they said: 'Are you friz?'
   He replied: 'Yes, I is,
But we don't call this cold in Quebec.'

Attributed to RUDYARD KIPLING
(1865–1936)

There was a young man of Devizes,
Whose ears★ were of different sizes;
   The one that was small
   Was no use at all,
But the other won several prizes.

ARCHIBALD MARSHALL
(1866–1934)

★ Anon. naturally prefers 'balls'.

There was a young man of Montrose,
Who had pockets in none of his clothes.
    When asked by his lass
    Where he carried his brass,
He said: 'Darling, I pay through the nose.'

ARNOLD BENNETT
(1867–1931)

An angry young husband called Bicket
Said: 'Turn yourself round and I'll kick it;
    You have painted my wife
    In the nude to the life.
Do you think, Mr Greene, it was cricket?'

JOHN GALSWORTHY
(1867–1933)

There was a young lady of Louth,
Who returned from a trip in the South;
    Her father said: 'Nelly,
    There's more in your belly
Than ever went in at your mouth.'

NORMAN DOUGLAS
(1868–1952)

There was a young fellow named Skinner,
Who took a young lady to dinner;
    At half-past nine
    They sat down to dine,
And by quarter to ten it was in her.
What, dinner?
No, Skinner.

NORMAN DOUGLAS

The ankle's chief end is exposiery
Of the latest designs in silk hosiery;
   Also, I suspect,
   It's a means to connect
The part called the calf with the toesiery.

ANTHONY EUWER
(1877–1955)

A wonderful bird is the pelican,
His bill can hold more than his belican.
   He can take in his beak
   Food enough for a week;
But I'm damned if I see how the helican.

DIXON MERRITT

Said a fair-headed maiden of Klondike:
'Of you I'm exceedingly fond, Ike.
   To prove I adore you,
   I'll dye, darling, for you,
And be a brunette, not a blonde, Ike.'

LANGFORD REED
(1889–1952)

A patriot living at Ewell
Found his bonfire wanted more fuel,
   So he threw in Uncle James
   To heighten the flames,
A measure effective though cruel.

LANGFORD REED

'I have heard,' said a maid from Montclair,
'Opportunity's step on the stair;
   But I couldn't unlock
   To its magical knock,
For I always was washing my hair.'

MORRIS BISHOP
(1893–1973)

Said a fervent young lady of Hammels:
'I object to humanity's trammels.
   I want to be free!
   Like a bird! Like a bee!
Oh, why am I classed with the mammals?'

MORRIS BISHOP

When a feverish groom in Armenia
Had nibbled away his gardenia,
   They just let him gaze
   On the bridesmaids' bouquets,
To quiet the old neurasthenia.

MORRIS BISHOP

G'uggery G'uggery Nunc
Your room is all cluttered with junk.
   Candles, bamboonery,
   Plush and saloonery –
Pack it all up in a trunk.

SIR JOHN BETJEMAN
(1906–1984)

There was an old gossip called Baird,
Who said: 'What I could say if I dared –
　　I will say it, in fact,
　　Though I die in the act.'
So she did, and nobody cared.

OGDEN NASH
(1902–1971)

There was a brave girl of Connecticut,
Who signalled the train with her pecticut;
　　Which the papers defined
　　As presence of mind,
But deplorable absence of ecticut.

OGDEN NASH

There was an old man of Calcutta,
Who coated his tonsils with butter;
　　Thus converting his snore
　　From a thunderous roar
To a soft oleagenous mutter.

OGDEN NASH

There was an old Bey of Calcutta,
Who greased his asshole with butter;
　　Instead of the roar
　　That came there before
Was a soft oleagenous mutter.

ANON.

The Postmaster-General cried: 'Arsehole!
A pair of bull's balls in a parcel!
   Stamped "I.R.A.",
   With ninepence to pay,
And addressed to the King, Windsor Castle!'

VICTOR GRAY
(b.1917)

A taxi-cab whore out at Iver
Would do the round trip for a fiver
   – Quite reasonable, too,
   For a sightsee, a screw,
And a ten-shilling tip for the driver.

VICTOR GRAY

A headstrong young lady of Ealing
Threw her two-year-old child at the ceiling;
   When quizzed why she did,
   She replied: 'To get rid
Of a strange overpowering feeling.'

EDWARD GOREY

To his club-footed child said Lord Stipple,
As he poured his post-prandial tipple:
   'Your mother's behaviour
   Gave pain to Our Saviour
And that's why He made you a cripple.'

EDWARD GOREY

Old Faithfuls

There was a young lady of Where?
Whose limerick likings most share;
   OLD FAITHFULS like these
    That are certain to please,
For they seem always to have been there.

There was a young man from Darjeeling,
Who got on a bus bound for Ealing;
   It said at the door:
   'Don't spit on the floor',
So he carefully spat on the ceiling.

ANON.

There was a young lady of Wantage,
Of whom the Town Clerk took advantage;
   Said the Borough Surveyor:
   'Of course you must pay her.
You've altered the line of her frontage.'

ANON.

There was a young lady of Joppa
Who came a society cropper;
   She went to Ostend
   With a gentleman friend –
And the rest of the story's improper.

ANON.

There was a young lady of Slough,
Who said that she didn't know how.
   'Till a young fellow caught her,
   And jolly well taught her,
And she lodges in Pimlico now.

ANON.

A young Irish servant in Drogheda
Had a mistress who often annogheda;
   Whereon she would swear
   In a language so rare,
That thereafter no-one emplogheda.

ANON.

There was a young man of Calcutta
Who had a most terrible stutta,
   He said: 'Pass the h. . .ham,
   And the j. . .j. . .j. . .jam,
And the b. . .b. . .b. . .b. . .b. . . . .butta.'

ANON.

There was a young lady called Maud,
A sort of society fraud;
   In the parlour, 'tis told,
   She was distant and cold,
But on the verandah, my Gawd!

ANON.

There was a young curate of Kew,
Who kept a tom cat in a pew;
   He taught it to speak
   Alphabetical Greek,
But it never got farther than μϋ

ANON.

There was a young lady called Starky,
Who had an affair with a darky;
   The result of her sins
    Was quads and not twins:
One white and one black, and two khaki.

ANON.

An innocent maiden of Gloucester
Fell in love with a coucester named Foucester;
   She met him in Leicester,
    Where he merely careicester,
Then the hard-headed coucester just loucester.

ANON.

The Honourable Winifred Wemyss
Saw styli and snakes in her dremyss;
   And these she enjeud
    Until she heard Freud
Say: 'Nothing is quite what it semyss.'

ANON.

'I must leave here,' said Lady De Vere,
'For these damp airs don't suit me, I fear.'
   Said her friend: 'Goodness me!
    If they don't agree
With your system, why eat pears, my dear?'

ANON.

'I must leave here,' said Lady De Vere . . .

There once was a lady called Lily,
With a craving to walk Piccadilly;
   She said: 'Ain't it funny?
   It's not to make money,
But men think my refusing it silly!'

ANON.

There was a young lady of fashion,
Who had oodles and oodles of passion;
   To her lover she said,
   As they climbed into bed:
'Here's one thing the bastards can't ration.'

ANON.

The new cinematic emporium
Is not just a super-sensorium,
   But a highly effectual
   Heterosexual
Mutual masturbatorium.

ANON.

A young girl of English nativity
Had a fanny of rare sensitivity;
   She could sit on the lap
   Of a Nazi or Jap,
And detect his Fifth Column activity.

ANON.

A tone-deaf old person of Tring,
When somebody asked him to sing,
  Replied: 'It is odd,
  But I cannot tell *God*
Save the Weasel from *Pop Goes the King*.'

ANON.

There was a young fellow of Lyme,
Who lived with three wives at one time.
  When asked: 'Why the third?'
  He replied: 'One's absurd,
And bigamy, sir, is a crime.'

ANON.

There was a young lady of Ryde,
Who ate some green apples and died;
  The apples fermented
  Inside the lamented,
And made cider inside her inside.

ANON.

In New Orleans dwelt a young Creole,
Who, when asked if her hair was all reole,
  Replied with a shrug:
  'Just give it a tug,
And decide by the way that I squeole.'

ALBEN BARKLEY

There was a young girl of Australia,
Who went to a dance as a dahlia;
   When the petals unfurled,
   It revealed to the world
That the dress, as a dress, was a failure.

ANON.

There was a young man of Australia,
Who painted his ass like a dahlia;
   The drawing was fine,
   The painting divine,
But the aroma – ah, that was the failure.

ANON.

A comely young widow named Ransom
Was ravished three times in a hansom;
   When she cried out for more,
   A voice from the floor
Cried: 'Lady, I'm Simpson, not Samson!'

ANON.

There was a young lady called Gloria,
Who was had by Sir Gerald Du Maurier,
   And then by six men,
   And Sir Gerald again,
And the band of the Waldorf-Astoria.

ANON.

There was a young fellow of Ceuta
Who rode into church on his scooter;
   He knocked down the Dean,
   And said: 'Sorry, old bean!
I ought to have sounded my hooter.'

ANON.

There was a young lady of Ealing,
Who walked up and down on the ceiling;
   She shouted: 'Oh, heck!
   I've broken my neck,
And it is a peculiar feeling.'

ANON.

There was an old man of Boulogne,
Who sang a most topical song;
   It wasn't the words
   Which frightened the birds
But the terrible 'double ontong'.

ANON.

A near-sighted fellow named Walter,
Led a glamorized lass to the altar;
   A beauty he thought her,
   Till some soap and water
Made her look like the Rock of Gibraltar.

ANON.

The Truth about Truth

THE TRUTH ABOUT TRUTH is elusive;
Is philosophy merely delusive?
   What seems rubbish to you
   May be for me true,
Which leaves everything inconclusive.

Simple living was clearly the nub
Of the teaching of one who could snub
   Alexander the Great
   With: 'Move along, mate!
You are taking the sun off my tub.'

JOYCE JOHNSON

Said Plato: 'The things that we feel
Are not ontologically real,
   But just the excrescence
   Of numinous essence
Our senses can never reveal.'

BASIL RANSOME-DAVIES

I was brought up on old Aristotle,
And won't change a jit or a tottle,
   And that's saying a lot,
   Not a jit, not a tot,
I *won't* alter – No, no, I'll nottle.

C.S.COOK

The Emperor Marcus Aurelius
Said that when we feel, it's not really us,
   Yet I rather suppose
   That a smack on the nose,
He'd have thought was a bit contumelious.

YORICK

There once was a man who said: 'God
Must think it exceedingly odd
 If He finds that this tree
 Continues to be,
When there's no-one about in the Quad.'
RONALD KNOX

[The Reply]

Dear Sir, Your astonishment's odd:
I am always about in the Quad.
 And that's why the tree
 Will continue to be,
Since observed by Yours faithfully, God.
ANON.

The philosopher Berkeley once said
In the dark to a maid in his bed:
 'No perception, my dear,
 Means I'm not really here,
But only a thought in your head.'
P.W.R.FOOT

There once was a man who said 'Damn!
It is borne in upon me I am
 An engine that moves
 In predestinate grooves;
I'm not even a bus, I'm a tram.'
M.E.HARE

There was a young student called Fred,
Who was questioned on Descartes and said:
  'It's perfectly clear
  That I'm not really here,
For I haven't a thought in my head.'

V. R. ORMEROD

Dr Johnson, when sober or pissed,
Could be frequently heard to insist,
  Letting out a great fart:
  'Yes, I follow Descartes –
I stink, and I therefore exist.'

A. CINNA

A toper who spies in the distance,
Striped tigers, will get some assistance
  From reading Descartes,
  Who holds that it's part
Of his duty to doubt their existence.

But if he's student of Berkeley,
One thing will emerge, rather starkly,
  That he ought to believe
  What his senses perceive,
No matter how dimly or darkly.

LESLIE JOHNSON

A Cynic says: 'Now that we know
Life's a futile incessant flow,
   And there's really no knowing
   The way it is going,
I am going to let myself go.'
THOMAS THORNELEY

When a man's too old even to toss off, he
Can sometimes be consoled by philosophy.
   One frequently shows a
   Strong taste for Spinoza,
When one's balls are beginning to ossify.
ROBERT CONQUEST

There was a young man who said: 'Ayer
Has answered the atheist's prayer,
   For a Hell one can't verify
   Surely can't terrify –
At least till you know you are there.'
ANON.

Said a practical thinker: 'One should
Help to kill superstition for good.
   I, for instance, refuse
   To observe all taboos,
With immunity, so far, touch wood.'
FRANK WATSON

Said an erudite sinologue: 'How
Shall I try to describe to you Tao?
  It is come, it is go,
  It is yes, it is no,
Yet it's neither – you understand now?'

R. J. P. HEWISON

Said the Stoic, tormented by gout:
'There are times when I'm tempted to doubt
  Our pose about pain,
  And disposed to complain
It is something we're better without.'

THOMAS THORNELEY

There was a professor of Beaulieu,
Who said mind was matter or ὕλη
  This contempt for the εἶδος
  Though common in Cnidos
Disturbed the New Forest unduly.

C. E. M. JOAD

There was a young girl of Shanghai,
Who was so exceedingly shy,
  That she undressed every night
  Without any light
Because of the All-Seeing Eye.

BERTRAND RUSSELL

Democracy works (*entre nous*) –
When a knowing intelligent few
   Tell the people: 'You rule!'
   And each plebeian fool
Says: 'Right, Guv'nor, what must we do?'

W. STEWART

Consistent disciples of Marx
Will have to employ special narks
   If nationalization
   Of all copulation
Leads to *laissez-faire* fucking in parks.

A. CINNA

When your capitalist boss takes his toll
You're a prole up the pole on the dole;
   Unite with your pal,
   For Dat's capital,
And then we'll have workers' control.

DOMINIC FITZPATRICK

Said a Marxist who stood on the pier:
'Though you may think my views rather queer,
   I could gambol all day
   With the sharks in the bay –
It's the ones in striped trousers I fear.'

W. H. G. PRICE

A man who had lately declared
That property ought to be shared,
   Thought it going too far
   When they called for his car,
And a list of exceptions prepared.

THOMAS THORNELEY

A hopeful old fellow called Rousseau,
Saw that man was not born bad, but grew so;
   If you change his surrounding,
   You'll find grace abounding –
You must turn the clock back to do so.

JOHN FAY

Said the Chinese philosopher, Lin:
'To trouble to work is a sin.
   In bed I shall stay,
   And the toil of the day
Will be finished before I begin.'

LEN

Don't think it will fall to your lot
To get what you like; it will not;
   But if you're heroic,
   And follow the Stoic,
You'll fancy you'll like what you've got.

LESLIE JOHNSON

Thomas Hobbes of Malmesbury thought
Life was nasty and brutish and short;
   But contracts, once made,
   Would come to our aid,
And ensure modest comfort – at court.

PETER ALEXANDER

Cried the maid: 'You must marry me, Hume!'
A statement that made David fume.
   He said: 'In cause and effect,
   There is a defect;
That it's mine you can only assume.'

P.W.R.FOOT

'If you're aristocratic,' said Nietzsche,
'It's thumbs up, you're O.K. Pleased to meitzsche.
   If you're working-class bores,
   It's thumbs down and up yours!
If you don't know your place, then I'll tietzsche.'

GERRY HAMILL

Said Wittgenstein: 'Don't be misled!
What *can* be shewn, cannot be said.'
   He aimed to be sensible,
   Not incomprehensible,
But wrote the *Tractatus* instead.

PETER ALEXANDER

Remember when you are bemusing,
And daily decisions confusing,
  That for life existential,
  The thing that's essential
Is never the choice but the choosing.

CYRIL HUGHES

I suppose I could try if I chose,
But the question is: 'Can I suppose
  I could *choose* what I chose if
  I chose?' I suppose if
I chose to. But nobody knows.

E.F.C.

The cryptic philosopher, Kant,
Announced: 'I most certainly shan't
  In my *Prolegomena*
  Allow that phenomena
Are anything but what they aren't.'

E.F.C.

An example of Kant's sterling wit
Was his theory that farts could be lit,
  And it's said that all night
  By the flickering light,
He composed his 'Critique of Pure Shit'.

VICTOR GRAY

A Solipsist with triplets said: 'Though
No-one else can exist, if it's so,
   Why I went through so much
   To bring up my clutch
In my fancy, I really don't know.'

LUPELLUS

The famous philosopher, Kant,
Said: 'Why, when I run, do I pant?
   I fear 'twould be treason
   To my *Critique of Reason*
To think I'm unfit, so I shan't.'

C.S.COOK

A candid Professor confesses
That the secret of half his success is
   Not his science, as such,
   Not its marvels so much
As his bright irresponsible guesses.

THOMAS THORNELEY

The United States Constitution
Owed a good deal to his contribution;
   This came as a shock
   In Heaven to Locke,
And he offered to make restitution.

PETER ALEXANDER

Theory and Practice

We all place a great deal of reliance
On the THEORY AND PRACTICE of science,
  But the hopeful intentions
  Of so many inventions
Can be quite buggered up in appliance.

There was a young lady called Bright
Who could travel far faster than light;
   She set off one day,
   In a relative way,
And returned home the previous night.

To her friends, said the Bright one, in chatter:
'I have learned something new about matter.
   My speed was so great
   That it increased my weight,
Yet I failed to become any fatter.'

A.H.R.BULLER

Albert Einstein's the man we must credit
For being the man who first said it.
   The name of the game
   That brought him his fame
Was $E = mc^2$ – Geddit?

STANLEY J. SHARPLESS

A fencing instructor named Fisk
In duel was terribly brisk;
   So fast was his action,
   The Fitzgerald Contraction
Foreshortened his foil to a disc.

ANON.

To Algebra God is inclined –
The world is a thought in His Mind.
  It seems so erratic
  Because it's quadratic,
And the roots are not easy to find.

J.C.B.DATE

An amoeba named Sam, and his brother
Were having a drink with each other;
  In the midst of their quaffing,
  They split themselves laughing,
And each of them now is a mother.

ANON.

A student from Pembroke once said:
'I'll take my mathematics to bed.
  My girl isn't willing,
  But I still want thrilling,
I'll integrate, quietly, instead.'

ANDREW STOKER

A man from Maputo and so on
Once kept a pet spermatozoon;
  It used to swim races
  In feminine places –
I haven't much data to go on.

J.H.LEE

Said philosopher-physicist Jeans:
'How many or few are five beans?
   Friend Einstein says four,
   Five, six, or more,
But I'm blowed if I know what he means.'

R.C.OWEN

Though Sir James (God's-a-Formula) Jeans
Holds the view that the stars are machines,
   He admits that behind
   The machine is a Mind,
– Or a Minder apparelled in Jeans?

R.J.P.HEWISON

A student of nuclear fission
Made a bomb with official permission;
   But the earth disappeared
   In the bang; it is feared,
Through an error in simple addition.

W. BERNARD WAKE

There once was a wise politician
Who said: 'I have faith in my mission;
   But if this bally bomb
   Kills the fellows it's from,
Then I'm placed in an awful position.'

A.M.SAYERS

Archimedes, the early truth-seeker,
Leapt out of his bath, cried 'Eureka!'
  And ran half a mile,
  Wearing only a smile,
Thus becoming the very first streaker.

STANLEY J. SHARPLESS

For travellers going sidereal,
The danger, they say, is bacterial.
  I don't know the pattern
  On Mars, or on Saturn
But on Venus it must be venereal.

ROBERT FROST

A binary mathematician
Had the curious erotic ambition
  To know what to do
  With the powers of two,
When the two are in proper position.

ANON.

Said a pupil of Einstein: 'It's rotten
To find I'd completely forgotten
  That by living so fast
  All my future's my past,
And I'm buried before I'm begotten.'

C. F. BEST

There was an old Doctor called Coué,
Who said to his patients: 'J'ai voué
   To cure all your ills
   Without any pills –
You just think yourself well – that's the new way!'

BOB SCOTT

There was a faith-healer of Deal
Who said: 'Although pain isn't real,
   If I sit on a pin,
   And it punctures my skin,
I dislike what I fancy I feel.'

ANON.

An ancient biologist, Heine,
Taught some girls that the female vagina
   Was the seat of their joy,
   But they shouted back: 'Oy!
We've got something much more divine!'

CAROL RUMENS

There once was an eccentric old boffin,
Who remarked, in a fine fit of coughing:
   'It isn't the cough
   That carries you off,
But the coffin they carries you off in.'

ANON.

A quirky old gent, name of Freud,
Was, not without reason, anneud
   That his concept of Id,
   And all that Id did,
Was so starkly and loosely empleud.

MARTIN FAGG

Said Freud: 'I've discovered the Id.
Of all your repressions be rid.
   It won't ease the gravity
   Of all the depravity,
But you'll know why you did what you did.'

FRANK RICHARDS

Sigmund Freud says that one who reflects
Sees that sex has far-reaching effects,
   For bottled-up urges
   Come out in great surges
In directions that no-one expects.

PETER ALEXANDER

'If you dream,' said the eminent Freud,
'Your Id is in doubt, or annoyed.
   By neuroses complex
   From suppression of sex,
So passions are best if enjoyed.'

RUSSELL MILLER

There was an old man called Dupree
Who couldn't count higher than three;
   He said 'Damn and God wot!
   It is plain I am not,
Because *si je pense, donc je suis.*'

R.I.

A cynical sage with a kink,
Said 'Between thought and deed there's a link;
   When I think what I thought,
   I don't do as I ought,
So it's best to do nought, and not think.

HASSALL PITMAN

[*Fundamentalism*]

Said a medical student, unmanned:
'Hellfire can't be properly planned.
   For all time to be doomed
   To burn on unconsumed,
Is what no constitution can stand.'

ALLEN M. LAING

There was an old lady of Leicester,
Whose numerous ailments obsessed her,
   She found no allure
   In an M. and B. cure,
And sedatives simply depressed her.

IAN T. MACKENZIE

A psychiatrist fellow from Rye
Went to visit another close by,
   Who said, with a grin,
   As he welcomed him in:
'Hullo, Smith! You're all right! How am I?'

STEPHEN CASS

Though your dreams may seem normal and right,
They bring horrible things to the light;
   You can only be sure
   That you're perfectly pure
If you dream about nothing all night.

J.C.B.DATE

According to old Sigmund Freud,
Life is seldom so well enjoyed
   As in human coition
   (In any position)
With the usual organs employed.

ANON.

An unfortunate lad from Madrid
Had both Super-Ego and Id,
   So whether he screwed,
   Or completely eschewed,
He felt guilty, whatever he did.

ANON.

Oedipus said to the Sphinx:
'My name's been perverted by shrinks.
　　Who'd think Jocasta'd
　　Call me a bastard?
I think psychiatry stinks.'

VICTOR GRAY

A sexy young student once toyed
With the Pelican series of Freud.
　　A new sense of mission
　　Brought dis-inhibition,
And her boy-friends were all overjoyed.

RICHARD TAYLOR

A young schizophrenic named Struther,
When told of the death of his brother,
　　Said: 'Yes, it's too bad,
　　But I can't feel too sad –
After all, I still have each other.'

ANON.

When an obstinate fellow of Fife
Insisted on loving his wife,
　　Denying obsessions,
　　And dreams and repressions,
The Freudians feared for his life.

ALLEN M. LAING

The people the Churches love best
Breed children like rabbits, with zest.
   They serve every passion
   In orthodox fashion,
The State gets the bill to digest.

PATRICK BRAYBROOK

There was a young fellow of Burma
Whose betrothed had good cause to murmur.
   But now that he's married he's
   Been using Cantharides,
And the roots of their love are much firmer.

ALDOUS HUXLEY

There was a young girl of East Anglia,
Whose loins were a tangle of ganglia,
   Her mind was a webbing
   Of Freud and Kraft-Ebbing.
And all sorts of other new fanglia.

ALDOUS HUXLEY

There was a young girl with a hernia
Who said to her doctor: 'Gol-dernia!
   When improving my middle
   Be sure you don't fiddle
With matters that do not concernia.'

HEYWOOD BROUN

There was a young Japanese geisha,
Who suffered from mild alopecia;
   She met a young Briton
   Identically smitten,
And they now run a barber's in Esher.

RON RUBIN

Whenever he got in a fury, a
Schizophrenic from Upper Manchuria,
   Had pseudocyesis,
   Disdiadochokinesis,
And haemotoporphyrimuria.

ANON.

A mosquito was heard to complain
That a chemist had poisoned his brain;
   The cause of his sorrow
   Was Para-dichloro-
Diphenyltrichlorothane.

ANON.

There was an old chap who said: 'Well,
I think my gout's giving me hell,
   But until one can find
   Which is Matter, which Mind,
How the hell is a fellow to tell?'

W. STEWART

These days, the ubiquitous db.
Reaches corners barely accb.;
   They say that it wrecks
   Many aspects of sex,
With results that are quite inexprb.

A.P.COX

A quadratic function, ambitious,
Said, 'It's not only wrong, but it's vicious.
   It's surely no sin
   To have max. and min.;
To limit me so is malicious.'

LEO MOSER

There once was a Fellow of Trinity,
Who raised XYZ to infinity.
   And then the old brute
   Extracted the root –
He afterwards took to divinity.

ANON.

There was a young man of Nepal
Who had a mathematical ball;
   $(W^3 \times \pi\,)) - 8 = \frac{4}{3}\sqrt{0}$
   (The cube of its weight
   Times Pi, minus eight
Is four thirds of the root of fuck all.)

ANON.

Wee Jamie, a canny young Scot,
Observed, when the kettle was hot,
  That the steam raised the lid,
  And it's thanks to this kid
That you and I know Watt's watt.

JOYCE JOHNSON

Watt's dream was the cream of steam engines.
Instead we get trains with a vengines.
  A lot of hot air,
  And 'Travellers' Fare' –
Was this his invengine's intengines?

BILL GREENWELL

George Stephenson said: 'These repairs
Are costing a fortune in spares.
  I'll be out of pocket
  When I've finished this Rocket,
Unless British Rail raise their fares.'

FRANK RICHARDS

Isaac Singer (you probably know)
Had a wish that his business should grow;
  But inventors before him,
  A few grudges bore him,
And thought him a real 'sew-and-sew'.

PETER BROOKES

[First Flight]

Said Wilbur Wright, 'Oh, this is grand,
But, Orville, you must understand.
   We've discovered all right
   The secret of flight –
The question is, how do we land?'

FRANK RICHARDS

Two earnest young fellows named Wright
Discovered the secret of flight.
   Now the earnest young crew
   Of a B52
Can wipe out the world overnight.

BASIL RANSOME-DAVIES

Said Orville to Wilbur 'Hold tight!
We're going to make our first flight.
   The ground we shall shift off.
   Hurrah! We have lift-off.'
And both of the brothers were Wright.

STANLEY J. SHARPLESS

A scientist living in Staines,
Is searching with infinite pains
   For a new sort of sound
   Which he hopes, when it's found,
Will travel much faster than planes.

R.J.P.HEWISON

79

'Come now,' said Bell, 'this is choice.
The first telephone! Let's rejoice!
  Now listen, folks all,
  To the very first call.'
'Sorry, number engaged,' said a voice.

FRANK RICHARDS

Exposing his plate to the air,
Did its clever inventor declare:
  '*C'est venue – ma photo,*
  Complète – in toto –
C'est magnifique – "Je suis Daguerre!"'

JOYCE JOHNSON

A calculus fit to compute on,
White light, and a head to drop fruit on,
  A mind to absorb it,
  And soar into orbit –
That's all that it takes to be Newton.

GINA BERKELEY

Marconi, whose ardour was tireless,
Sat down and invented the wireless,
  Which makes it less tough
  For the musical buff
Who lives in a town that is choir-less.

STANLEY J. SHARPLESS

History's Mysteries

In HISTORY'S MYSTERIES vast,
The present's as strange as the past,
    But before you condemn,
    Remember – *pro tem* –
You also are one of the cast.

Consider the Emperor Nero –
Of many lewd tales he's the hero –
  Though he scraped on the fiddle,
  He just couldn't diddle –
And his *real* batting average was zero.

ANON.

I, CAESAR, when I learned of the fame
Of Cleopatra, I straightway laid claim.
  Ahead of my legions,
  I invaded her regions –
I saw, I conquered, I came.

ANON.

Boadicea often would goad
Some chance soldier she met on the road,
  Then paint with isatis★,
  Their sex apparatus,
And embrace, crying: 'One for the woad!'

DOUGLAS CATLEY

I wonder how King Arthur felt,
When one day Queen Guinevere knelt,
  Saying: 'Tell me, my pet,
  How did Lancelot get
The key of my chastity belt?'

MOSS RICH

★ *Isatis tinctoria* is the botanical name for the plant from which woad was extracted.

'Strip,' Leofric said, 'and you'll find
I'll take off the tax you've in mind.'
  So Godiva, she streaked,
  And nobody peeked,
Except Peeping Tom, who went blind.

HARRY THOMAS

A crusader's wife slipped from the garrison
And had an affair with a Saracen;
  She was not over-sexed,
  Or jealous or vexed,
She just wanted to make a comparison.

OGDEN NASH

There was a crusader of Parma,
Who went to bed with his charma;
  She, naturally nude,
  Said: 'Don't think me rude,
But do you think you should take off your arma?'

ANON.

[*King Richard II*]
King Richard, in one of his rages,
Forsook his good lady for ages,
  And rested in bed
  With a good book instead,
Or, preferably, one of the pages.

A. B. HALL

There once was a monarch called Harry,
Whose efforts seemed doomed to miscarry,
  Since his wish for a son,
  Plus unlimited fun,
Made him marry and marry and marry.

MARY HOLTBY

King Henry the Eighth was a Tudor,
Of our monarchs we've witnessed fu ludor;
  Each wife that he wed,
  He led to the bed,
Where he vudor, and wudor, and scrudor.

KIRKHAM TALBOT

To his Queen said the circumspect Burleigh:
'It is true that you are old Harry's girlie,
  But if you meet Essex
  And do not suppress sex
You'll be had by the short and the curly.'

A. CINNA

The immaculate Sir Walter Raleigh
Had a terrible row with his valet,
  Who, on seeing his cloak,
  Cried: 'You lousy old soak,
You've been rolling about in the alley.'

T. L. MCCARTHY

It is clear that Napoleon's Queen
Was referring to army routine,
  When she said, in a flummox,
  'Marchons-nous sur nos stomachs?'
And was told, 'Not tonight, Josephine.'

MOSS RICH

Said Nelson at his most la–di–da–di:
'I am sorry, if I seem rather tardy,
  But I face a dilemma –
  Should I bugger my Emma
Or screw the delectable Hardy?'

A. CINNA

Said Wellington: 'What's the location
Of this battle I've won for the nation?'
  They replied: 'Waterloo.'
  He said: 'That'll do.
What a glorious name for a station.'

FRANK RICHARDS

The wily Napoleon Bonaparte
Took powerful Louis's plush throne apart,
  But the weak Josephine
  With her frontal fur screen
And central attack, took Nap's stones apart.

DOUGLAS CATLEY

Victoria was bitterly short
About hanky-panky at court;
   One lady admonished,
   Said: 'I am astonished.
John Brown cannot be what I thought.'
CYRIL MOUNTJOY

'We're not amused,' said Victoria,
In a mood far removed from euphoria,
   But a visit from Dizzy
   Put her in a tizzy
And her views grew Tory-er and Tory-er.
STANLEY J. SHARPLESS

'Dear Albert, of Saxe-Coburg-Gotha,
We desire to receive our due quota
   Of amorous sport,
   And not be kept short
By one tittle, or jot, or iota.'
W.F.N. WATSON

Said the Queen to her favourite ghillie,
In a voice that was notably chilly:
   'While we don't wish to quarrel,
   We don't think it's Balmoral,
What you're doing to us with your willy.'
A. CINNA

'We're not amused,' said Victoria . . .

[General Gordon Speaks]

'Some people may think I'm a bit la-di-
Da, others say I'm quite hardy;
    The truth is, in brief,
    I'm seeking relief
But not at the hands of the Mahdi.'

C. VITA-FINZI

'No more mistresses,' King Edward said,
'Now gardening's my hobby instead.
    Now, don't think this silly,
    I've this nice Jersey Lily,
All ready to put into a bed.'

FRANK RICHARDS

'What have I done?' said Christine:
'I've ruined the party machine.
    To lie in the nude
    Is not very rude,
But to lie in the House is obscene.'

ANON.

There was an old sage of New Delhi,
Who said: 'When you're kicked in the belly,
    By a neighbouring tribe,
    Don't browbeat or bribe –
Be Nehru, not Machiavelli.'

JOYCE PARR

What led to the crassness of Custer,
With hardly a unit to muster?
  At the little Big Horn,
  Sitting Bull gave a yawn,
And said: 'You're a sitting duck, buster!'

BILL GREENWELL

George Washington said to his dad:
'You know that big fruit-tree you had?
  I've just chopped it down –
  Now, father don't frown –
I can't tell a lie. Aren't you glad?'

FRANK RICHARDS

[*Presentiment About a President, 1968*]

Is there really a new Mr Nixon,
Who won't try his previous tricks on?
  Or is it a fact
  That he's virgin intact
When it comes to a stand by conviction.

T. GRIFFITHS

In the days of mild Jerry Ford,
Decorum and calm were restored;
  He did nothing hateful,
  For which we were grateful,
And terribly, terribly bored.

ANON.

Ronald Reagan screamed out in dismay,
When he saw his old films: 'I must say
  It's a very hard fact –
  I must learn to act.'
And that's what he does every day.

FRANK RICHARDS

A General once lived named de Gaulle,
Five hundred years old, ten yards tall.
  He thought he was God,
  Which was really quite odd,
For God's David Frost, if at all.

PAUL BRISTOW

There was a great Marxist called Lenin,
Who did two or three million men in;
  That's a lot to have done in,
  But where he did one in,
That great Marxist Stalin did ten in.

TED PAUKER

The trouble with General Sherman –
He acted too much like a German –
  Attacking Savannah
  In much the same manner
As Adolf or Heinrich or Hermann.

BASIL RANSOME-DAVIES

An earnest young leftie named Tariq,
Blackballed when put up for the Garrick,
   Observed with a groan:
   'These balls are my own,
I consider your conduct barbaric.'

BERNARD LEVIN

Said Paisley: 'I've given up hope,
The world's on a mad slippery slope;
   What a farce they have made
   Of my brilliant crusade,
For I've been nominated as Pope.'

FRANK RICHARDS

Said Powell: 'Don't call me insane.
My policy's perfectly plain,
   And not at all similar
   To that of Herr Himmler –
My final solution's humane.'

ROGER WODDIS

[*A Mental Reservation, 1927 – de Valera Speaks*]

'Sign your name in the book. It's just ink.
It won't hurt you. Now, let's have a drink!
   We'll build a new nation
   On this reservation.
Fianna Fail. By the right – double think!'

SYDNEY BERNARD SMITH

Said the famous philosopher, Russell:
'One can come without moving a muscle.
  When sufficiently blotto,
  Just watch Lady Otto-
line's bum as it bursts from her bustle.'
VICTOR GRAY

Prince Charles in his Welsh principality
Formed a violent left-wing sodality;
  When asked why this was
  He replied: 'It's because
I am sick of the family mentality.'
BERNARD LEVIN

There was a young monarch called Ed,
Who took Mrs Simpson to bed;
  As they bounced up and down,
  He said: 'Bugger the crown!
We'll give it to Albert instead.'
ANON.

The last time I slept with the Queen,
She said, as I whistled '*Ich Dien*':
  'It's royalty's night out,
  But please put the light out,
The Queen may be had, but not seen.'
DYLAN THOMAS

From the elephant paddock one day,
They took poor Barbara Woodhouse away;
   There's no harm, in the least,
   Shouting 'Sit' to the beast,
But she should have got out of the way.

FRANK RICHARDS

Mrs Whitehouse, mixed bathing at Deal,
Emitted a loud piercing squeal,
   It seems she had fingered
   A something that lingered –
And certainly wasn't an eel.

T. L. MCCARTHY

Said a God-fearing lady called Whitehouse:
'I am going to retire to a lighthouse,
   Where never is heard
   A four-letter word,
And nobody calls you a shitehouse.'

ROGER WODDIS

Rupert Murdoch, with glee, shouted: 'What
A lot of newspapers I've got!
   I've just got to get
   The *Beekeepers' Gazette*
And the *War Cry* and I've got the lot.'

FRANK RICHARDS

There was an old Member called Bevan
Who wanted to make Britain Heaven;
　　When they said: 'You will fail.'
　　He replied: 'Ebbw Vale
Gives the strength to its children of seven.'

BARBARA LEIGH

A rather extreme vegetarian
Looked down from his summit Bavarian;
　　He said: 'It's not odd
　　I'm superior to God,
For the latter is not even Aryan.'

SAGITTARIUS

Viscount Stansgate, or Wedgwood, or Benn
(Three in one to the left-minded men)
　　Says 'Issues are all,
　　Generalities pall,
But I'm there if you want me – say when.'

TIM HOPKINS

Said Tebbitt: 'I don't understand 'em.
If they really want jobs, they can land 'em.
　　If a work-seeking tyke
　　Has no luck on a bike,
He can double his chance on a tandem.'

GERRY HAMILL

Clerical Errors

Though CLERICAL ERRORS are fun,
The Bishops decree there are none,
  Or else they infer
  That if they occur
They must never be seen to be done.

There was a young curate of Salisbury,
Whose manners were quite halisbury-scalisbury;
   He walked about Hampshire
   Without any pampshire,
Till his Vicar obliged him to walisbury.

ANON.

There was a young curate of Hants,
Who suddenly took off his pants,
   When asked why he did,
   He replied: 'To get rid
Of this terrible army of ants.'

E.V.KNOX

A complacent old Don of Divinity,
Made boast of his daughter's virginity:
   'They must have been dawdlin',
   The students of Magdalen;
It couldn't have happened at Trinity.'

ANON.

A cleric once heard with dismay
Each week he worked only one day.
   He said, with a sigh:
   'I cannot think why
I'm so busy on days when I play.'

JOAN DARE

A modern young curate called Hyde,
Will be pleased if the bishops decide
   That, to govern a see,
   One must hold a degree
In Evil, both pure and applied.

D.W.PAIN

'The conception,' an Archbishop said,
'Of a *personal* Tempter is dead.'
   But a meek little curate
   Begged leave to demur; it
Was something he fought with in bed.

L.E.J.

There once was a Scot who said: 'Evil
Is a relic of thoughts medieval:
   Those tales of Auld Nick
   And his power make me sick.
It's just being Guid that's the devil!'

H.M.

Said a parson, addressing his flock:
'So-called Progress is in for a shock.
   We've *intuitive proofs*
   Of a Devil-with-hoofs –
Which will put back the clock before Locke.'

W.J.STRACHAN

A divine by the name of McWhinners
Held classes each evening for sinners,
  They were sectioned and graded
  So the very de-graded
Would not be held back by beginners.

ANON.

There was an old person of Fratton,
Who would go to church with his hat on.
  'When I wake up,' he said,
  'With my hat on my head,
I shall know that it hasn't been sat on.'

ANON.

There was a young lady called Alice,
Who peed in a Catholic chalice.
  The Padre agreed
  It was done out of need,
And not out of Protestant malice.

ANON.

There was a young monk from Siberia,
Whose morals were very inferior;
  He did to a nun
  What he shouldn't have done,
And now she's a Mother Superior.

ANON.

There was a young lady of Chichester
Who made all the saints in their niches stir;
   One morning at Matins,
   Her breasts, in white satins,
Made the Bishop of Chichester's britches stir.

                        ANON.

There was a young fellow called Baker,
Who seduced a vivacious young Quaker;
   And when he had done it,
   She straightened her bonnet,
And said: 'I give thanks to my Maker.'

                        ANON.

A Salvation lassie named Claire
Was having her first love affair.
   As she climbed into bed,
   She reverently said:
'I wish to be opened with prayer.'

                        ANON.

A handsome young monk in a wood
Told a girl she should cling to the Good.
   She obeyed him, but gladly,
   He repulsed her, but sadly,
And said she had misunderstood.

                        ANON.

The sermon our Pastor, Rt. Rev.,
Began, may have had a rt. clev.,
  But his talk, though consistent,
  Kept the end so far distant,
That we left, as we felt he mt. nev.

ANON.

There was a young priest of Dun Laoghaire,
Who stood on his head in the *Kyrie*;
  When people asked why,
  He said in reply:
'It's the latest liturgical theory.'

ANON.

There was a young lady of Tottenham,
Her manners – she'd completely forgotten 'em;
  While at tea at the vicar's,
  She took off her knickers,
Explaining she felt much too hot in 'em.

ANON.

There once was a vicar of Ryhill,
Who went for a shit on a high hill;
  When his Curate asked: 'Was it
  A goodly deposit?'
He said: '*Vox, et praetera nihil.*'

ANON.

From the crypt of the church of St Giles,
Came a cry that resounded for miles;
    Said the vicar, 'Good gracious!
    Has Father Ignatius
Forgotten the Bishop has piles?'

ANON.

There was a young maiden of Devon,
Who was raped in the garden by seven
    High Anglican priests –
    The lascivious beasts!
Of such is the Kingdom of Heaven.

ANON.

A desperate spinster of Clare,
Once knelt in the moonlight all bare,
    And prayed to her God
    For a romp in the sod –
A passer-by answered her prayer.

ANON.

There's a fortunate priest of St Paul's,
Has demountable penis and balls;
    These, for urgent appeals
    And the nuns' meals-on-wheels,
He can send out on house-to-house calls.

DOUGLAS CATLEY

When our dean took a pious young spinster
On his cultural tour of York Minster,
   What they did in the clerestory,
   Is rather a queer story –
But none of us hold it aginster.

VICTOR GRAY

There was a young curate called Lloyd,
Who was seldom, if ever, annoyed;
   Although you might poke him,
   You could never provoke him –
His *sang* was so terribly *froid*.

Attributed to DUNCAN CAMPBELL McGREGOR

An indolent vicar of Bray
His roses allowed to decay;
   His wife, more alert,
   Bought a powerful squirt,
And said to her spouse: 'Let us spray.'

LANGFORD REED

The Reverend Mr Uprightly
Was cuckolded daily and nightly;
   He murmured: 'Dear, dear!
   I would fain interfere,
If I knew how to do it politely.'

ANON.

A minister up in Vermont
Keeps a goldfish alive in his font;
   When he dips the babes in,
   It tickles the skin,
Which is all that the innocent want.

ANON.

'Given faith,' sighed the vicar of Deneham,
'From the lusts of the flesh we might wean 'em;
   But the human soul sighs
   For a nice pair of thighs,
And a little of what lies beween 'em.'

ANON.

There once was a wicked young minister,
Whose conduct was thought to be sinister;
   By ruses nightmarish
   He seduced the whole parish,
Except for one squeamish old spinister.

CONRAD AIKEN

Astute Melanesians on Munda
Heard a Parson discussing the wunda
   Of Virginal Birth –
   They debated its worth,
Then tore the poor Padre asunda.

ANON.

On the Way Out

There isn't a shadow of doubt
We're all of us ON THE WAY OUT,
   From old age or ambition
   Of excessive coition –
So drink up before you are nowt.

There was a young lady of Riga,
Who smiled as she rode on a tiger:
   They returned from the ride
   With the lady inside,
And the smile on the face of the tiger.

COSMO MONKHOUSE

A young man by a girl was desired
To give her the thrills she required;
   But he died of old age
   Ere his cock could assuage
The volcanic desires it inspired.

ANON.

A boastful young fellow of Neath
Once hung from the roof by his teeth;
   A very large crowd
   First cheered him quite loud,
Then passed round the hat for a wreath.

FRANK RICHARDS

The babe with a cry, brief and dismal,
Fell into the waters baptismal;
   Ere they'd gathered its plight,
   It had sunk out of sight,
For the depths of that font were abysmal.

EDWARD GOREY

From the bathing-machine came a din
As of jollification within;
   It was heard far and wide
   And the incoming tide
Had a definite flavour of gin.

EDWARD GOREY

Pulmonary Tuberculosis
Is all very well in small doses,
   But a gap in the lung
   As big as a bung,
Means years while you twiddle your toeses.

L.G.UDALL

There was a young fellow called Clyde
Who once at a funeral was spied.
   When asked who was dead,
   He smilingly said:
'I don't know – I just came for the ride.'

ANON.

There was an old cynic who said:
'Though I don't despise colds in the head,
   I get no real thrill
   Till I'm dangerously ill,
With friends eating grapes round my bed.'

ALLEN M.LAING

There was a young fellow called Hall,
Who fell in the spring in the fall;
   'Twould have been a sad thing,
   Had he died in the spring,
But he didn't, he died in the fall.

ANON.

As the natives got ready to serve
A midget explorer named Merve;
   'This meal will be brief,'
   Said the cannibal chief,
'For this is at best an *hors d'oeuvre.*'

ED CUNNINGHAM

A serious young lady from Welwyn
Took a cookery-book up Helvellyn;
   While reading the recipes
   She fell off a precipice,
And that was the end of poor Ellen.

C. ARMSTRONG GIBBS

A jolly young fellow from Yuma
Told an elephant joke to a puma;
   Now his skeleton lies
   Beneath hot western skies –
The puma had no sense of huma.

OGDEN NASH

There was a young fellow named Fisher
Who was fishing for fish in a fissure;
   Then a cod, with a grin,
   Pulled the fisherman in . . .
Now they're searching the fissure for Fisher.
ANON.

Said a boastful young student from Hayes,
As he entered the Hampton Court Maze:
   'There's nothing in it.
   I won't be a minute.'
He's been missing for forty-one days.
FRANK RICHARDS

A maiden at college called Breeze,
Weighed down by B.A.s and Litt.D.s,
   Collapsed from the strain
   Alas! It was plain
She was killing herself by degrees.
MRS WARREN

An amorous maiden antique
Kept a man in her house for a week;
   He entered her door
   With, a shout and a roar,
But his exit was marked by a squeak.
ANON.

An unpopular man of Cologne
With a pain in his stomach did mogne;
   He heaved a great sigh,
   And said: 'I would digh,
But the loss would be simply my ogne.'

ANON.

A careless explorer named Blake
Fell into a tropical lake.
   Said a fat alligator,
   A few minutes later:
'Very nice, but I still prefer cake.'

OGDEN NASH

Said a foolish young lady of Wales:
'A smell of escaped gas prevails.'
   Then she searched with a light,
   And later that night,
Was collected in several pails.

LANGFORD REED

Said the vet as he looked at my pet:
'That's the skinniest bear that I've met.
   I'll soon alter that.'
   Now the bear's nice and fat –
The question is – where is the vet?

FRANK RICHARDS

There was an old fellow named Hewing,
Whose heart stopped while he was a-screwing;
 He gasped: 'Really, Miss,
 Don't feel bad about this –
There's nothing I'd rather die doing.'

ANON.

The Hoover, in grim silence, sat,
But sucking no more at the mat;
 Quietly it grunted
 As slowly it shunted,
And messily disgorged the cat.

DAVID WOODSFORD

If intercourse gives you thrombosis,
And continence causes neurosis,
 I'd rather expire
 Fulfilling desire
Than live in a state of psychosis.

ANON.

From Number Nine, Penwiper Mews,
There is really abominable news:
 They've discovered a head
 In the box for the bread,
But nobody seems to know whose.

EDWARD GOREY

There was a young fellow from Tyne
Put his head on the South-Eastern line;
   But he died of *ennui*,
    For the 5.53
Didn't come till a quarter past nine.

ANON.

An artist who lived in St Ives
Collected quaint African knives;
   But his children all thought,
    They were bought for their sport –
Out of eight only one now survives.

A.G.PRYS-JONES

There was a young lady called Harris,
That nothing could ever embarrass;
   Till the bath-salts one day
    In the tub where she lay
Turned out to be plaster of Paris.

OGDEN NASH

A certain young gourmet of Crediton
Took some *pâté de foie gras* and spread it on
   A chocolate biscuit,
    Then murmured: 'I'll risk it.' –
His tomb bears the date that he said it on.

CHARLES CUTHBERT INGE

There was a young lady of Ryde
Who was carried too far by the tide;
   Cried a man-eating shark:
   'How's this for a lark?
I knew that the Lord would provide.'

ANON.

A retired Civil Servant from Gateley,
Who lived in a home known as stately,
   Kept lions, for fun,
   In a wire netting run,
But he hasn't been seen around lately.

IDA THURTLE

An elderly bride of Port Jervis
Was quite understandably nervis,
   Since her apple-cheeked groom,
   With three wives in the tomb,
Kept insuring her during the servis.

OGDEN NASH

An incautious woman called Venn,
Was seen with the wrong sort of men;
   She vanished one day,
   But the following May,
Her legs were retrieved from a fen.

EDWARD GOREY

There was a young fellow named Fonda
Who was squeezed by a great anaconda;
   Now he's only a smear,
   With part of him here,
And the rest of him somewhere out yonder.

OGDEN NASH

There once was a doctor who said:
'Far too many sick folk die in bed:
   There's no deadlier place
   And to rescue the race,
I suggest using armchairs instead.'

TOWANBUCKET

There was an old man who averred
He had learned how to fly like a bird;
   Cheered by thousands of people,
   He leapt from the steeple –
This tomb states the date it occurred.

ANON.

A daring young lady of Guam
Observed 'The Pacific's so calm.
   I'll swim out for a lark.'
   She met a large shark –
'Let us now sing the Ninetieth Psalm.'

ANON.

The Literary Scene

Let's enter THE LITERARY SCENE,
The whole world of might-have-been,
 But it's best to recall,
 Before having a ball,
What's Literature can't be obscene.

There was a young fellow of Trinity,
Who, although he could trill like a linnet, he
   Could never complete
   Any poem with feet,
Saying: 'Idiots!
      Can't you see
      What I'm writing
        happens
        to be
  Free
  Verse?'

ANON.

There was a young man of Japan,
Who wrote verses that never would scan.
   When folk told him so,
   He replied: 'Yes, I know,
But I always try and get as many words into the
   last line as I possibly can.'

ANON.

There was a young poet of Kew,
Who failed to emerge into view;
   So he said: 'I'll dispense
   With rhyme, metre and sense.'
And he did, and he's now in *Who's Who*.

ANON.

When approached by a person from Porlock,
It is best to take time by the forelock.
  Shout: 'I'm not at home,
   'Till I've finished this pome!'
And refuse to unfasten the door-lock.

RICHARD LEIGHTON GREENE

Shelley's death – was it really his wish
To be drowned 'midst Italian fish?
  I certainly think
  I'd dive in the drink
If my parents had christened me Bysshe.

BILL GREENWELL

When Keats was at work on *Endymion*,
He suddenly shouted: 'Oh, gimme an
  Unashamed naked nereid
  From the Ancient Greek period,
Not just Fanny Brawne, with her shimmy on.'

VICTOR GRAY

[*The Morning After Audience Participation*]
  I haven't a clue where I've been.
  There were recriminations and spleen.
   I feel kind of crabby,
    'Twas maybe the Abbey –
  (I think I created a scene.)

SYDNEY BERNARD SMITH

T. S. Eliot is quite at a loss
When clubwomen bustle across
  At literary teas,
   Crying: 'What, if you please,
Did you mean by *The Mill on the Floss*?'
W. H. AUDEN

A scribe, to the vulgar inclined,
Wrote a play more gross than refined,
  With words, all four-letter:
   Hips, nips, tits, and better
Like those that have just crossed your mind.
DOUGLAS CATLEY

It's a pity that Casabianca
Was using his tool as an anchor;
  If he'd had it up higher,
   He'd have put out the fire,
You never did see such a wanker.
VICTOR GRAY

Victoria said: 'We've no quarrel
With Shakespeare, but this is immoral!
  His *Measure for Measure*
   Incurs our displeasure;
We don't do such things at Balmoral.'
FRANK RICHARDS

A Novelist, flushed with success,
Said: 'The World's in a horrible mess.
  With its quarrels it needs
  The new morals and creeds
I shall shortly be sending to press.'

THOMAS THORNELEY

A famous theatrical actress
Played best in the role of malefactress.
  Yet her home-life was pure,
  Except, to be sure,
A scandal or two just for practice.

ANON.

There once was a writer called James,
Whose ways with Bostonian dames
  Was to take them from home
  To Paris or Rome
For dubious linguistical games.

R. K. R. THORNTON

Said a famous old writer called Fender:
'You may think that my conscience is tender,
  You may think that my heart
  Is my most sensitive part,
But you should see my poor old pudenda.'

VICTOR GRAY

Said Old Nick: 'Mister Lewis and me
Is the best pals that ever was, see?
   We both has our loyalties,
   We both share the royalties –
I've a very warm corner for he!'

M.CASSEL

Said Arnold to Arthur Hugh Clough:
'Why I don't instantly stuff
   Your *Amours du Voyage*
   Up my arse is it's large,
But I don't think it's quite large enough.'

VICTOR GRAY

An artist who lived near Montmartre
Made improper suggestions to Sartre,
   But Sartre, with a blow
   At his hanging *huis clos*,
Cut his two existentials apartre.

SIR JOHN WALLER, Bt.

There was a young man of Cape Race,
Whose mind was an utter disgrace;
   He thought Marie Corelli
   Lived long before Shelley,
And that Wells was the name of a place.

ANON.

There was a young man of Newcastle,
Who thought of himself as a parcel;
   Which he'd tied with red tape,
   And addressed, for a jape,
To: 'What Hope? c/o Kafka, The Castle.'

TERENCE MELICAN

How Socratic is Somerset Maugham!
What is virtue to him but a norm?
   So the best propaedeutic
   Is a process maieutic,
And all evil is merely bad form.

R. B. S. INSTONE

Let the eugenist reach for his gun!
Would Keats have been Keats if A. I.?
   And the world better off
   With a healthy Van Gogh,
And a clean-living, right-thinking Donne?

STANLEY J. SHARPLESS

A publisher went off to France,
In search of a tale of romance;
   A Parisian lady
   Told a story so shady
That the publisher made an advance.

ANON.

That smasher of shams, Bernard Shaw,
Points out to the Sophists the flaw
   In each flattering unction,
   And, lacking compunction,
Makes hay of the drowning man's straw.

                FRANK BUCKLAND

Ninety summers – and never a platitude,
Or a single uncivilized attitude;
   Ebullient heir
   Of Sam Butler, Voltaire,
Would you mind if we mention our gratitude?

              STANLEY J. SHARPLESS

O sage of the stage, Shaw of Shaws!
As your victims we venture applause.
   Too ascetic for Paris,
   Not to mention Frank Harris,
Your Webb-footed genius awes.

              HAROLD ELLIS

All his life, Mr George Bernard Shaw
Has enjoyed catching fools on the raw;
   At ninety we find
   There's no change in his mind,
Or decay in the set of his jaw.

              AUDREY HERBERT

There was a kind lady called Gregory
Said: 'Come to me, poets in beggary.'
  But found her imprudence
  When thousands of students
Cried: 'All we are in that category.'

JAMES JOYCE

A filthy young fellow called Lawrence
Poured out torrid titles in torrents,
  Offending the spouses
  Of well-to-do houses,
Whilst their servants were filled with abhorrence.

BILL GREENWELL

'Political women,' thought Yeats,
'Have come to be top of my hates.'
  His views rested on
  His love of Maud Gonne,
Who wouldn't go out on his dates.

R. K. R. THORNTON

A novelist of the Absurd
Has a voice that will shortly be heard;
  I learn from my spies
  He's about to devise
An unprintable three-letter word.

OGDEN NASH

Two playwrights called Beaumont and Fletcher,
Sent a coach to a strumpet to fetch her;
  For they lived as they wrote,
  Sometimes sharing a coat,
And always both sharing a lecher.

FIONA PITT-KETHLEY

That fine English poet, John Donne,
Was wont to admonish the Sunne:
  'You busie old foole,
  Lie still and keep coole,
For I am in bed having funne.'

WENDY COPE

A rebuke by the Bishop of London
To his randy young dean, Dr John Donne:
  'In the Name, Sir, of God, peace,
  If you won't wear a cod-piece,
Don't preach with your fly-buttons undone.'

VICTOR GRAY

An English professor named Brooks
Said: 'Reviewing is not what it looks;
  Now I always choose
  To review the reviews
Of the books about writers of books.'

D.H.CUDMORE

Mr Wells of the big cerebellum
Uses mountains of paper or vellum;
   When his temper gets bad
   And we ask 'Why go mad?'
He replies: 'They won't do as I tell 'em.'

                        H.G.WELLS

Our novels get longa and longa;
Their language gets stronga and stronga;
   There's much to be said
   For a life that is led
In illiterate places like Bonga.

                        H.G.WELLS

The Marquis de Sade and Genet
Are most highly thought of today;
   But torture and treachery
   Are not his sort of lechery,
So he's given his copy away.

                     W.H.AUDEN

Charlotte Brontë said: 'Wow, sister! *What* a man!
He laid me face down on the ottoman:
   Now don't you and Emily
   Go telling the femily,
But he smacked me upon the bottom, Anne!'

                    VICTOR GRAY

A budding young playwright named Coward
Came into the Twenties and flowered.
  He continued to sparkle
  Until the Debacle:
Now the fruit is a teeny bit soured.

DORIS PULSFORD

Mr Alan Jay Lerner (with by-play)
Made *Pygmalion* less of a dry play;
  Seraph Shaw, near hysterics,
  On hearing his lyrics,
Shocked Heaven with: 'Not bloody my play!'

J. A. LINDON

In Pinter's new play that's now running,
Our Harold's lost none of his cunning.
  Throughout the three acts,
  We hear just four facts,
But the pauses between are quite stunning.

FRANK RICHARDS

[*On the Proposed Founding of an Irish Academy*]

G. B. Shaw wrote to Yeats: 'P'raps it's mad of me
And I know that you folks will think bad of me,
  But may I remark,
  Before you embark,
That I *am* the Irish Academy.'

W. A. RATHKEY

A budding young playwright named Coward . . .

An authoress, armed with a skewer,
Once hunted a hostile reviewer.
  'I'll teach him', she cried,
  'When I've punctured his hide,
To call my last novel too pure.'

ANON.

There once was a couple named Mound,
Whose sexual control was profound;
  When engaged in coition,
  They had the ambition
To study the *Cantos* by Pound.

ANON.

Said Tennyson: 'Yes, *Locksley Hall*'s
A story that always enthralls,
  For it comes down to this –
  She gave me a kiss,
And then a good kick in the balls.'

VICTOR GRAY

'I would doubt,' said the Bishop of Balham,
'If Tennyson ever had Hallam.
  Such things are best hid.
  Let's hope that he did
De mortuis nil nisi malum.'

TERENCE RATTIGAN

There was a young poet of Thusis,
Who went twilight walks with the Muses,
  But the nymphs of the air
  Are not what they were,
And the practice has led to abuses.

ANON.

If you find for your verse there's no call,
And you can't afford paper at all,
  For the poet true born,
  However forlorn,
There's always the lavatory wall.

ANON.

Ivy Compton-Burnett's irritations,
And the titles she gives her narrations,
  All these misses and misters,
  All those 'Brothers and Sisters' –
They all sound like sexual relations.

ANON.

A wily old writer called Maugham
Was seldom, if ever, off faugham,
  His works were incisive,
  And often derisive,
But really his heart was quite waugham.

MARTIN FAGG

A FEW FOR THE POT

[*'All the world's a stage. . .'*]

Seven ages, first puking and mewling,
Then very pissed off with one's schooling,
   Then fucks, and then fights,
   Then judging chaps' rights;
Then sitting in slippers; then drooling.

                   VICTOR GRAY

[*'Here with a loaf of bread. . .'*]

'A book and a jug and a dame,
And a nice cosy nook for the same.
   And I don't give a damn,'
   Said Omar Khayyam,
'What you say, it's a great little game.'

                       ANON.

[*'O what can ail thee. . .'*]

'What's the matter, old chap?' 'Well, I came
Just by chance on this good-looking dame.
   All was fine, till she got
   Me inside her old grot –
Since which, I have not been the same.'

                JOYCE JOHNSON

[*'I wandered lonely as a cloud. . .'*]

I spotted these daffs by the lake.
And a right pretty picture they make.
   Because of these flowers,
   I'm dreaming for hours –
Which gives my libido a break.

                E. O. PARROTT

[D. H. Lawrence, *Lady Chatterley's Lover*]

The gamekeeper of Lady Chatterley
Was rewarded more often than qua'terly.
  'Though I feel quite a beast,'
  She reflected, 'At least,
I'm having it off more than latterly.'

GERRY HAMILL

[Shakespeare, *Titus Andronicus*]

A man called Andronicus (Titus),
Had a nasty attack of colitis;
  It began with meat pies,
  And the issuing cries
Of his sons saying: 'Daddy, don't bite us.'

PAUL WIGMORE

[Charlotte Brontë, *Jane Eyre*]

Mr Rochester's wife's pyromania
Made him hanker for someone unzanier.
  'No, no!' said the parson.
  But, after more arson,
A little voice whispered: 'It's Jane here!'

GINA BERKELEY

[James Joyce, *Ulysses*]

While Dubliner leopold bloom sought solace
from thoughts of the tomb in daedalic mazes his moll went to blazes
and dreamed
a great yes in her room.

GERARD BENSON

[R. L. Stevenson, *Dr Jekyll and Mr Hyde*]

There once was a fellow called Hyde,
Whose twin self he couldn't abide;
   But Jekyll, the Devil,
   Dragged Hyde to his level,
'Inside job,' cried Hyde, as he died.

E. J. JACKSON

[James Joyce, *Finnegans Wake*]

Riverrun where can you guess?
Finnegans Wake is a mess
   Will you help me get even
   Said left-over Stephen
Yes I said yes I will Yes.

ANON.

[Shakespeare, *Othello*]

Othello loved Desdemona,
But wrongly thought Cassio'd known her;
   When a hankie went missing,
   There was an end to the kissing,
He snuffed her, then regretted his boner.

A. CINNA

[Shakespeare, *Hamlet*]

Did Ophelia ask Hamlet to bed?
Was Gertrude incestuously wed?
   Is there anything certain?
   By the fall of the curtain
Almost everyone's certainly dead.

A. CINNA

[Shakespeare, *Hamlet*]

Prince Hamlet thought uncle a traitor
For having it off with his Mater;
   Revenge Dad or not –
   That's the gist of the plot –
And he did – nine soliloquies later.
STANLEY J. SHARPLESS

[John Keats, *Isabella*]

Both Keats and Boccaccio tell a
Sad tale about Isabella
   Who was worn to a frazzle
   Weeping over some basil
That grew in the skull of her fella.
JOYCE JOHNSON

[Hilaire Belloc, *Tarantella*]

Miranda, remember that Inn?
Where we drank that tart wine from the skin?
   Then we slept in the straw
   Where the fleas made us sore
And the peasantry made such a din.
JOHN STANLEY

[Dylan Thomas, *Under Milk Wood*]

Night's bible-black darkness prevails
In a small seaside village in Wales;
   Where the neighbours have dreams
   That burst out at the seams,
To reveal some immodest details.
V. R. ORMEROD

[Robert Browning, *The Pied Piper of Hamelin*]

Having rid Hamelin town of its vermin,
And been tricked by a noddy in ermine;
   He lured girls and boys
   With his pipe's pleasant noise
Where they went, not a soul can determine.

TED THOMPSON

[Edgar Allan Poe, *The Raven*]

Once a raven from Pluto's dark shore
Brought the singular news: 'Nevermore.'
   'Twas of useless avail
   To ask further detail,
His reply was the same as before.

ANTHONY EUWER

[Jean Ingelow,
High Tide on the Coast of Lincolnshire]

The bells from the steeple resound,
As the flood waters spread all around;
   When they ebbed at the dawn
   My poor boy was forlorn,
His dear Liz, and the kids, had been drowned.

JOHN STANLEY

[James Joyce,
Portrait of the Artist as a Young Man]

When Ireland was bloody and leaderless,
The tedious, garrulous Daedalus –
   Having failed both as priest
   And as Glorious Beast –
Sailed away to write books that were readerless.

GINA BERKELEY

[T. S. Eliot, *Burnt Norton*]

In dealing with time it is found
That the future and past move around.
  So the present is cast.
  In the future and past.
It seems we are breaking new ground.

                    V. R. ORMEROD

[T. S. Eliot,
The Lovesong of J. Alfred Prufrock]

An angst-ridden amorist, Fred,
Saw sartorial changes ahead.
  His mind kept on ringing
  With fishy girls singing.
Soft fruit also filled him with dread.

                    J. WALKER

[Samuel Coleridge,
The Rime of the Ancient Mariner]

No, listen, there's this albatross,
I shot him, he wasn't half cross.
  He had the crew cursed, he
  Made us feel thirsty.
I'm ancient now. Tragic, eh, boss?

                    BILL GREENWELL

[Thomas Gray, *Elegy in a Country Churchyard*]

When I sit in the Churchyard at Stoke,
I reflect – Class is merely a joke.
  Elsewhere I can pass
  As good upper class,
But here I'm just one of the folk.

                    A. M. SAYERS

GONERIL/REGAN: Pop's tops!

LEAR: True, Cordelia?

CORDELIA: Oh, *Dad!*

LEAR: I banish you!

KENT: Gad!

LEAR: Vanish!

FOOL: Mad!
Believe me, these sisters
Deceive you,

LEAR: The twisters!

GLOUCESTER: And my boy's a bastard.

EDMUND: Too bad.

EDGAR: I'm disguised. Tom's a fruitcake.

LEAR: Me too!

GONERIL/REGAN: Prise those eyes out.

GLOUCESTER: I'm blinded! Boo-hoo!

EDMUND: I fix my own odds.

GLOUCESTER: The gods are such sods.

EDGAR: No they're not. Jump! All right!

GLOUCESTER: And that's true.

REGAN: My hubby's just snuffed it. To bed!

EDMUND: My lady?

GONERIL: He's mine!

ALBANY: You're still wed.

LEAR: The law is an ass;
Forgive me, my lass.

CORDELIA: Of course!

REGAN: Ugh!

GONERIL: Agh!

EDMUND: Oogh!

ALBANY: They're all dead!

ALBANY:	Good old gods! Three cheers!
KENT:	I feel queer!
LEAR:	She's dead. Howl. Fool. Gurgle.
ALBANY:	Oh dear!
KENT:	He's dead and I'm dying.
EDGAR:	It's time to start crying;
	I'm king. That's your lot. Shed a tear.

BILL GREENWELL

[Rupert Brooke, *The Old Rectory, Grantchester*]

O, I yearn to go back to the Cam!
For nostalgic is just what I am!
   To the Backs turn my back
   And then notice the lack
Of honey – 'Is there only jam?'

Is it two-fifty still on the ticker?
Won't time ever go any quicker?
   And after a jar
   Will I see *pas de chat*
From a Terpsichorean vicar?

Do chestnuts still bloom by the river,
With lilacs and pinks all a-quiver?
   Will I be bolder
   Now that I'm older
And beer-drinking has ruined my liver?

E. O. PARROTT

[G. M. Hopkins, *The Wreck of the Deutschland*]

A boat-load of emigrant Huns,
Including five death-destined nuns;
   Came to grief on a shoal,
   But since Heaven's our goal,
The dead were the fortunate ones.

DAVID ANNETT

[William Wordsworth, *Intimations of Immortality*]

In childhood it's easy to feel
The eternal suffusing the real,
   But as the beholder
   Gets steadily older,
It doesn't seem such a big deal.

NIGEL ANDREW

[W. B. Yeats, *Easter, 1916*]

There was a collection of schemers,
Who swore they were going to redeem us.
   I said 'No, you're not'
   But now they've been shot.
The heroes! The darlings! The dreamers!

BASIL RANSOME-DAVIES

[T. S. Eliot, *The Waste Land*]

April. Bad month. Visit spa.
Play chess. Meet too fecund Mamma.
   Look on undismayed
   While typist gets laid.
Jug Jug. Da. Damyata. Ta ta.

STANLEY J. SHARPLESS

THE WORLD OF FICTION

[*Yorick*]

An old Danish jester named Yorick
Drank a gallon of pure paregoric;
   'My jokes have been dull,'
   He said, 'but my skull
Will one of these days be historic.'

OGDEN NASH

[*Miranda*]

A randy young girl called Miranda,
Wanted laying by someone much grander
   Than an ill-favoured chump
   Who was nearly all hump,
And so Ferdinand easily manned her.

PETER ALEXANDER

[*Ophelia*]

Poor Ophelia sighed: 'I deplore
The fact that young Hamlet's a bore.
   He just talks to himself;
   I'll be left on the shelf,
Or go mad by the end of Act IV.'

FRANK RICHARDS

[*Philip Marlow*]

Said Marlowe: 'Bay City's a drag
And no place to go for a jag.
   When I find a nice dame
   Who remembers my name,
There's always a rod in her bag.'

PETER ALEXANDER

[*Lady Chatterley*]

Her husband was *hors de combat,*
But she didn't have to look very far
   For suitable fellers,
   The gamekeeper, Mellors,
Provided the *non sine qua.*

C. VITA-FINZI

[*Orsino*]

In Illyria, the love-sick Orsino
Sighed: 'Why is her answer to me "No"?'
   A theme he'd rehearse
   At length in blank verse –
Not a part, one would think, for Dan Leno.

STANLEY J. SHARPLESS

[A Postscript to Orwell's *Animal Farm*]

There once was a child who said: 'How
A spider, a goose, and a cow
   Can have equal delights
   And identical rights,
Without civil war, or a row?'

Dear Child, you will surely allow
Sound sense in our reasoning now;
   Though each equals me,
   I'm more equal than he.
So I'm boss.
   Yours contentedly,
         Cow.

MIADESNIA

A man in the Land of the Houyhnhnms,
Had a large collection of antohnhnms;
   He would say: 'This is great!
   They're in pairs, so they mate,
Unlike synohnhnms, and, of course, homohnhnms.'

W. S. BROWNLEE

A lecherous young Lilliputian
Made advances, his feet on a cutian;
   But, although fully erect,
   He failed to connect,
However hard he was putian.

C. VITA-FINZI

When an amorous youth from Atlantis
Removed an Amazon's παντις
   And dragged her to bed,
   She cut off his head,
But he carried on just like a mantis.

C. VITA-FINZI

When Pegotty found Barkis was willing,
She really went in for a killing;
   When she left the bed,
   Poor Barkis was dead,
And up with the angels, re-filling.

DOUGLAS CATLEY

The Dickensian borough of Coketown
Would get any sensitive bloke down;
   The rigidly trad mind
   Of rigid T. Gradgrind
Is geared to make liberal folk frown.

MARTIN FAGG

A Fellow from far Erewhon,
With girl students did well, as a don,
   For an alpha, he said,
   A romp on the bed
Was almost a *sine qua non*.

W.F.N.WATSON

The feminine mouth in Utopia
Would rival a Greek cornucopia,
   Which is Nature's wise plan,
   Since Utopian man
Is a martyr to chronic myopia.

W.F.N.WATSON

Said a girl in green Mansfield Park:
'Our Jane is away! What a lark!
   Unlike with Miss Austen,
   We'll have beaux accostin' –
And more, if they're up to the mark.'

E.O.PARROTT

There was a young lady called Muffet
Who sat spooning whey on a tuffet,
   When a hairy arachnid
   In terms coarse and hackneyed,
Succinctly enjoined her to stuff it.

AUTHOR UNKNOWN

The inept young person, Miss Muffet,
Had further bad luck with her tuffet;
   Some used-tuffet dealers
   Decided to steal hers,
So now she must hire one – or rough it.

DEAN WALLEY

An Unperson from West Oceania
For self-whipping developed a mania;
   Picture then his elation
   At the Thought-Police Station,
When they said: 'Give it up – or we'll cania.'

C. VITA-FINZI

'Princess,' said the Frog, 'do not wince:
I'll convince you I'm really a prince!'
   So he changed – into tights –
   And demanded his rights,
And nobody's heard of him since.

GINA BERKELEY

There was a young boy, Jack Horner,
Who played with his plums in the corner;
   Said his father: 'That's bad.
   When I was a lad,
I preferred a massage down the sauna.'

FIONA PITT-KETHLEY

A platinum blonde, Goldilocks,
Who kept a *ménage* near the docks,
   Had it off with three bears
   Near Wapping Old Stairs,
And infected them all with the pox.

FIONA PITT-KETHLEY

The fact of the matter is, Jack
Had long wanted Jill on her back;
   So he told her some tale
   About filling a pail,
And then bungled his plan of attack.

JOHN STANLEY

A lady from Vanity Fair
Had a most astonishing pair;
   One listing to port
   Was the usual sort,
But the other, to starboard, was square.

W.F.N.WATSON

The fabulous Wizard of Oz
Retired from business becoz
   What with up-to-date science,
   To most of his clients,
He wasn't the Wizard he woz.

ANON.

There was a young outlaw named Hood,
Who lived in a Nottingham wood;
   He learned how to fuck
   From old Friar Tuck,
And made Marian whenever he could.

E. O. PARROTT

There was a young princess, Snow-White,
Who awoke with a terrible fright
   She was frightened and shaken –
   She shouldn't have taken
That Seven-Up last thing at night.

GERARD BENSON

Said Old Father William: 'I'm humble,
And getting too old for a tumble,
   But produce me a blonde,
   And I'm still not beyond
An attempt at an interesting fumble.'

CONRAD AIKEN

Last Christmas, when Puss was in Boots,
He met a young tabby called Toots;
   They looked at a condom
   But found it beyond 'em,
So what do you bet on the fruits?

GINA BERKELEY

There once were two Babes in the Wood
Who happened to meet Robin Hood,
   Who said, with a leer:
   'Would you think it queer
If I stuffed you with turkey and pud?'

ROGER WODDIS

The Old Woman who lived in the Shoe
Whacked all her kids black and blue;
   If only she had
   Seen an F. P. A ad,
Then she would have known what to do.

JOYCE JOHNSON

When the Prince, who was terribly smit,
Tried the slipper on Cinders, and it
   Fitted so snugly,
   It gave the two Ugly
Old Sisters a worse kind of fit.

JOYCE JOHNSON

POETIC FANCIES

[*Tennyson*]
The rose gives a tremulous glance,
And sighs: 'He is lost in a trance!'
  'Let us wait,' cries the pink,
  'He is coming, I think'
But the passion flower weeps: 'Not a chance.'
ANNE NORRIS

Her limp lover Maud couldn't pardon
He was no use at all in the garden;
  But drooped like the rose,
  When the sap in it goes.
''Ere, Enoch,' she cried, 'Enoch, 'arden!'
KIT WRIGHT

There once was a lass of Shalott,
Who was put in a bit of a spot;
  For girls to make passes
  At guys glimpsed in glasses
Apparently isn't so hot.
MARY HOLTBY

William McGonagall, *Patriotic Address
from the Banks of the Silvery Tay*

O Great Queen Whom I idolize,
'Twould be a most pleasant surprise
  And one to remember
  Could I place my Member
Between thy Mighty and Sovereign thighs.
JEFFREY LITTMAN

[*G. M. Hopkins*]

The heart of O'Leary, S.J.
Stirred for a bird in the hay,
  So he side-saddled Lily,
  Fair fire-freckled filly,
And rode her long-lustly all day.

DAVID PHILLIPS

[*A. E. Housman*]

A Salopian student of Greek
Had a love of Hellenic physique;
  And many a lad
  In Ludlow he had,
By the dint of his classic technique.

MARTIN FAGG

[*Edward Fitzgerald*]

An old poet called Omar cried: 'Now
I've found Paradise truly, and how!
  I regret what I've said –
  Stuff verse, wine and bread!
I'll have thou and have thou and have thou!'

J.E.C.

[*A Tribute to Matthew Arnold
in a Moment of Self-Abuse*]

A scholar of Oxford, while tipsy,
Began to make love to a gipsy;
  He undressed her, caressed her,
  To the beach he had pressed her,
Then found he'd lost faith in his ipse.

RICHARD SHEPHERD

[Robert Browning, *The Last Ride Together*]

'Is it thou?' 'Ay,' cries Fra Lippo Lippi,
''Zooks, lass, 'tis confoundedly nippy.
  But slip out of your gown
  And I'll give you a crown
Or two more, but we'd best make it slippy.'

So they up and went at it like knives,
Or they humped (shall I say it?) 's though their lives
  Were dependent on what
  They performed and they got
To the climax in just twenty drives.

Of the loins. She sighed: '*Flower of the vine*,
My God! You are perfectly mine.
  'Tis enough. Keep your gold
  But, my love, I grow cold.
Where's 'e gone? Where's my gown? Brrr, you swine!'

GERARD BENSON

[*Geoffrey Chaucer*]

Ther once was this ladye from Tyre,
Whoo fild evry mann with dees sire;
  Tenn quid was enuf
  For your back sete stuf,
But fees for onne nite were much hyer.

TIM HOPKINS

Sound and Vision

The Limerick lacks the precision
To evaluate all SOUND AND VISION;
   Yellow bricks in a pile,
   Or a sonata for file,
Require an aesthetic decision.

A concert conductor in Rio
Fell in love with a lady called Cleo;
   As she took down her panties,
   He said: 'No *andantes*!
I want it *allegro con brio*!'

ANON.

There was a trombonist called Herb,
Whose playing was loud (though superb);
   When neighbours complained,
   Young Herbert explained:
'But great art is meant to disturb.'

RON RUBIN

The young things who frequent picture-palaces
Have no time for psychoanalysis,
   And though Dr Freud
   Is distinctly annoyed
They cling to their long-standing fallacies.

PHILIP HESELTINE

As Mozart composed a sonata,
The maid bent to fasten her garter;
   Without any delay
   He started to play
Un poco piu appassionata.

ANON.

A musical maiden from Frome,
Allowed a friend's fingers to roam,
　　He taught her the score,
　　Then gave an encore
On her other erogenous dome.

CYRIL BIBBY

Said Isolde to Tristan: 'How curious!
Old Mark is becoming quite furious.
　　Since we got off that boat,
　　It's been all *Liebestod*.
Is it possible Wagner is spurious?'

CONRAD AIKEN

Of a sudden, the great prima donna
Cried: 'Gawd: my voice is a gonner.'
　　But a cat in the wings
　　Said: 'I know how she sings,'
And finished the solo with honour.

ANON.

There's a sensitive type in Tom's River
Whom Beethoven causes to quiver;
　　The aesthetic vibration
　　Brings soulful elation,
And also is fine for the liver.

ANON.

There was a young fellow called Cager,
Who, as the result of a wager,
   Offered to fart
   The whole oboe part
Of Mozart's *Quartet in F Major.*

ANON.

A certain young man of Hilgay
Took his harp to a concert one day;
   The audience cheered,
   When on stage he appeared,
But they groaned when he started to play.

IDA THURTLE

A Victorian gent said: 'This dance,
The can-can, which we've got from France,
   Fills me with disgust –
   It generates lust –
You should see it while you have the chance.'

FRANK RICHARDS

'Tis strange how the newspapers honour
A creature that's called prima donna;
   They say not a thing
   Of how she can sing,
But write reams of the clothes she has on her.

EUGENE FIELD

A modern composer called Cage
For silence became all the rage.
　　No performer, he found,
　　Ever made the wrong sound,
Or misread the notes on the page.

PETER ALEXANDER

One midnight, old D. G. Rossetti
Remarked to Miss Sidall: 'Oh, Betty,
　　I wish that you'd stop
　　Shouting "Fuck me, you wop!"
It turna da tool to spaghetti!'

VICTOR GRAY

There once was an artist called Pat,
Who carried her paints in her hat,
　　Friends said: 'It appears
　　From the state of your ears
That your ultramarine is squashed flat.'

MARGARET GALBREATH

There was a young artist called Saint,
Who swallowed some samples of paint;
　　All shades of the spectrum
　　Flowed out of his rectrum
With a colourful lack of restraint.

ANON.

[Stanley Spencer, 'Resurrection']

The conclusion I reach at the Tate
When I stand by this work and debate
   On the stiffs easing out,
   Is that quite without doubt,
They are all of them going to be late.

TALLIS

[Dante Gabriel Rossetti, 'Lady Lilith']

What! Parted! Not even a kiss?
Pray, what is the meaning of this?
   I declare it's not fair!
   I shall tear out my hair,
And *next* time I'll be done by Matisse!

X.A.M.

There once was a flock of wild geese,
Whose numbers were on the increase;
   Remarked Peter Scott:
   'I must paint the whole lot,'
Which he did – and still does without cease.

B. and C. SEMEONOFF

[*A Renoir*]

There was a young woman who said:
'My cheeks are so round and so red,
   And the light on my dress
   Is like pure happiness,
In the shade of the apple-tree spread.'

FRANCES CORNFORD

[Jan van Eyck, 'The Arnolfinis']

Arnolfinis both sat to Van Eyck;
Said the wife: 'Though it's ugly, it's like.
   Even if the truth mattered,
   I'd rather be flattered.
Why didn't we wait for Van Dyck?'

SIR ROBERT WITT

[Meindert Hobbema, 'The Avenue, Middleharnis']

I consider I really am through
With Hobbema's Dutch Avenue;
   The trees are so tall,
   Their tops are so small,
And they utterly ruin the view.

ELIZABETH H. LISTER

[Peter Paul Rubens, 'The Rape of the Sabines']

Of attractions the Sabines ain't stinted;
And I tell you my eyes fairly glinted;
   At the toes and the knees,
   The those and the these –
But hist! or I'll never be printed.

D. W. BARKER

'Monsieur Gauguin? 'E's gone to Tahiti,
Where ze girls are so friendly and pretty;
   'E paints them *tout* bare,
   Wiz zair lovely black 'air,
And bodies zo – 'ow you say? "meaty"!'

STANLEY J. SHARPLESS

Whilst Titian was mixing rose madder,
His model posed nude on a ladder;
   Her position to Titian
   Suggested coition,
So he climbed up the ladder and had her.

ANON.

There once was a sculptor named Phidias
Who had a distate for the hideous;
   So he sculpt Aphrodite
   Without any nightie,
Which shocked the ultra-fastidious.

ANON.

An ascetic art student named Josh
Said: 'Artistic licence won't wash!
   My models wear tights
   For Worldly Delights
Are a lot of Hieronymous Bosch.'

D. H. CUDMORE

The smile on the famed Mona Lisa
Has long been a bit of a teaser;
   Perhaps Leonardo
   In a fit of bravado
Made as if he were going to squeeze her.

STANLEY J. SHARPLESS

For his Campbell's Soup screen-prints, society's
Wild about Warhol. In quiet, he's
  Wishing that Heinz
  Had inspired his designs –
He'd have 57 varieties.

BILL GREENWELL

Far beyond all the girls of Pirelli
Are the females of S. Botticelli;
  Each has porcelain skin,
  And a pert pointed chin,
And erogenous botti and belli.

I. D. M. MORLEY

A ballistical student named Raffity
Went down to the Gentlemen's laffity;
  When the walls met his sight,
  He said; 'Newton was right.
This must be the centre of graffity.'

D. H. CUDMORE

Said the Duchess of Alba to Goya:
'Paint some pictures to hang in my foya!'
  So he painted her twice:
  In the nude, to look nice,
And then in her clothes, to annoya.

ANON.

One morning the Monarch said: 'When
May I hope for a Queen of the Glen?
   I look noble, I'm sure,
   But my thoughts are not pure –
I'm no better than most other men.'

D. W. BARKER

[Walter Sickert, 'Ennui']

There we was, and wanting our tea,
And him painting Hubby and me;
   My, we was bored!
   They showed it abroad,
And now they call it 'On We'.

P.E.A.

Van Gogh, feeling devil-may-care,
Labelled one of his efforts 'The Chair'.
   No-one knows if the bloke
   Perpetrated a joke,
Or the furniture needed repair.

PIBWOB

Is it really so very unthinkable
That Rodin's 'The Thinker' is linkable
   To the desperately cool
   Meditation at stool,
When one knows that one's passed an unsinkable?

BASIL RANSOME-DAVIES

A sculptor remarked: 'I'm afraid
I have fallen in love with my trade,
  I'm much too elated
  With what I've created,
But chiefly the women I've made.'

                    ANON.

A mordant and decadent Youth
Said: 'Beauty is greater than Truth.
  But by Beauty I mean
  The obscure, the obscene,
The diseased, the decayed, the uncouth.'

          THOMAS THORNELEY

'The figure is not anatomical,'
Said the Sitter, 'the attitude's comical.'
  Said the Painter: 'Quite true,
  But looked at askew,
Both are seen to be sweetly symbolical.'

          THOMAS THORNELEY

A Painter, encumbered with cash,
Said: 'It's time to be making a splash.
  I can paint, if I care,
  Things to startle and scare,
Though I'm fully aware they are trash.'

          THOMAS THORNELEY

Cakes and Ale

In considering things gastronomic,
CAKES AND ALE are not quite economic;
   Though maybe we oughter
   Stick to plain bread and water,
It's gin makes a tonic a tonic.

An epicure, dining at Crewe,
Found a rather large mouse in his stew;
  Said the waiter: 'Don't shout,
  Or wave it about,
Or the rest will be wanting one too.'

ANON.

There was a young man of Ostend
Who went for a drink with a friend;
  They had a few jars
  With two boys in some bars,
And so each had a friend in the end.

E. O. PARROTT

There was a young lady of Trent,
Who said that she knew what it meant
  When men asked her to dine
  With cocktails and wine,
She knew what it meant – but she went.

ANON.

Not that it always transpired
That it turned out quite as she desired;
  One gent of Trent
  Was undoubtedly bent,
And he didn't advance – he retired.

CYRIL RAY

A glib little beer-buff from Troon
Says slim girls will cause him to swoon;
   A girl with no waist
   Is of course to his taste,
With his gut like a busted balloon.

BILL GREENWELL

There was an old drunkard of Devon,
Who died and ascended to Heaven;
   But he cried: 'This is Hades –
   There are no naughty ladies,
And the pubs are all shut by eleven.'

RON RUBIN

There was an old man in a trunk
Who inquired of his wife: 'Am I drunk?'
   She replied with regret:
   'I'm afraid so, my pet.'
And he answered: 'It's just as I thunk.'

OGDEN NASH

There was a young lady at court
Who said to the King, with a snort:
   'Was it humour or shyness
   That prompted your Highness
To put Spanish Fly in my port?'

D. H. CUDMORE

[*Inishbofin Local Reconditioned*]

A very apt question struck me;
The answer's not easy to see,
   But now that that door
   Isn't there any more,
Just where do we go for a pee?
SYDNEY BERNARD SMITH

On the chest of a barmaid in Sale
Were tattooed the prices of ale,
   And on her behind,
   For the sake of the blind,
Was the same information in Braille.
ANON.

There was an old drunk called Hieronymus,
Who joined Alcoholics Anonymous;
   But with liver disease,
   The shakes and D. T.s,
The prognostication is ominous.
RON RUBIN

There was a young girl whose frigidity
Approached cataleptic rigidity,
   Till you gave her a drink,
   When she quickly would sink
In a state of complaisant liquidity.
ANON.

I went with the Duchess to tea,
Her manners were shocking to see;
   Her rumblings abdominal
   Were simply phenomenal,
And everyone thought it was me.

WOODROW WILSON (?)

When I thought of this Duchess affair,
It suddenly struck me: 'How rare
   Are abnormal vitals
   In ladies with titles,
So I'm glad after all I was there.'

ANON.

The Dowager Duchess of Spout
Collapsed at the height of a rout;
   She found strength to say
   As they bore her away:
'I should never have taken the trout.'

EDWARD GOREY

There was a young man so benighted
He didn't know when he was slighted;
   He went to a party,
   And ate just as hearty
As if he'd been really invited.

FRANCES PARKINSON KEYES

I was sitting there, taking my ease,
And enjoying my Beaumes-de-Venise,
   With a charming young poppet,
   But she told me to stop it
As my fingers crept up past her knees.

CYRIL RAY

There was a young girl of St Cyr,
Whose reflex reactions were queer;
   Her escort said: 'Mabel,
   Get up off the table!
That money is there for the beer.'

ANON.

The exquisite bartender at Sweeney's
Is famed for his ale and free wienies,
   But I thought him uncouth
   To gulp gin and vermouth,
Chill the glasses and piddle Martinis.

ANON.

A scion of Boston society
Was pinched, and for mere insobriety.
   'I will lay in the gutter,
   Refusing to utter
One word in defence of sobriety.'

CONRAD AIKEN

There was a young fellow named Sydney,
Who drank till he ruined his kidney.
   It shrivelled and shrank
   And he sat there and drank,
But he had a good time of it, didn'e?

DON MARQUIS

There was a young man of Porthcawl
Who thought he was Samson or Saul;
   These thoughts so obscure
   Were due to the brewer,
And not to his ego at all.

A. G. PRYS-JONES

'At last I've seduced the *au pair*
With some steak and a chocolate eclair,
   Some peas and some chips,
   Three Miracle Whips,
And a carafe of *vin ordinaire*.'

CYRIL RAY

'COME TO NOAH's for wine and strong waters,
And for diddling in clean classy quarters.
   I assure every guest
   I've made personal test
Of my booze and my beds and my daughters.'

ANON.

There was an old man of Dundee,
Who came home as drunk as can be;
   He wound up the clock
   With the end of his cock,
And buggered his wife with the key.

                                    ANON.

A man who was asked out to dinner,
Came home looking hungry and thinner;
   He said: 'Don't look baffled,
   The dinner was raffled,
And somebody else was the winner.'

                          SPIKE MILLIGAN

Well, if it's a sin to like Guinness,
Then that I admit's what my sin is.
   I like it with fizz,
   Or just as it is,
And it's much better for me than gin is.

                             CYRIL RAY

Sardines seem to get out of hand
In a way I can not understand;
   For they never appear
   At the table, I hear,
Unless they are tight, oiled and canned.

                        LESLIE JOHNSON

An old gourmet who's grown somewhat stout,
Felt a twinge and much feared it was gout.
  'If I drink now,' he thought,
  'Three whole bottles of port,
It surely will settle the doubt.'

YORICK

If you feel that you're right on your beam ends,
If your gait is more rolling than seamen's,
  And if camels in helmets
  March over the pelmets,
You've a touch of *delerium tremens*.

LESLIE JOHNSON

Said a herring one day to a sole:
'Life's very unfair – 'pon my shoal!
  While I'm stark on a slab,
  You will be with that crab,
Billed in French at the Ritz-Metropole.'

STANLEY J. SHARPLESS

It's a nightmare that horrifies hakes
To finish as frugal fish-cakes;
  But O, what a dream
  To be stewed slow in cream,
Or fresh-fried in respectable steaks!

ALLEN M. LAING

Unworldly Affairs

The Limerick realm now prepares
For some rather UNWORLDLY AFFAIRS;
   It's of course, melancholy
   That not all gods are holy,
But have lusts that each mortal man shares.

[Deus 'Sex' Machina]

An ingenious god was old Zeus,
He assumed many forms to seduce,
   So any Greek beauty
   Would think it her duty
To submit to a swan – or a goose.

To share faithful Alcmena's bed,
Jove's disguise was the man she'd wed;
   But this husbandly mould
   Left the good wife quite cold,
'Not tonight dear, my head aches,' she said.

Europa was awed, and was pawed
By a bull, who was Zeus, her lord;
   As he fled with his prize,
   He pronounced this disguise
A divine way to ride abroad.

To pent Danae, Zeus of old,
Appeared as a shower of gold;
   When he'd made her surrender
   To his legal tender,
'Oh, please keep the change,' he was told.

HARRIET MANDELBAUM

When a friend said to Leda: 'Come on,
Tell me why you are looking so wan?'
    She replied: 'It's inspiring,
    But ever so tiring
When a girl has it off with a swan.'

PETER ALEXANDER

Said Mars when entangled with Venus:
'I think there is something between us,
    And the sound in my ears
    Of Olympian jeers,
Suggests that the blighters have seen us!'

MARY HOLTBY

My demands upon life are quite modest:
They're just to be properly goddessed;
    Astarte or Isis
    Might do in a crisis,
But the best's Aphrodite, unbodiced.

ROBERT CONQUEST

'How much,' sighed the gentle Narcissus,
'A man of my character misses!
    It's clear on reflection,
    I've got an erection,
But all I can do is blow kisses.'

STEPHEN SYLVESTER

Cassandra declining to follow
His amorous leanings, Apollo,
   Exceedingly miffed,
   Allowed her the gift
Of predictions that no-one would swallow.

BASIL RANSOME-DAVIES

Young Oedipus learned from the Sphinx
He was under a terrible jinx;
   He would – no, I can't tell
   All the rest that befell –
It's not family reading. It stinks.

BASIL RANSOME-DAVIES

Few things to desire can so prod us,
As much as a plump Hindu goddess,
   With eight clinging arms
   And exuberant charms
That are never concealed in a bodice.

W.F.N.WATSON

'For the tenth time, dull Daphnis,' said Chloe,
'You have told me my bosom is snowy;
   You have made much fine verse on
   Each part of my person,
Now *do* something, there's a good boy!'

ANON.

A lady, who signs herself 'Vexed',
Writes to say she believes she's been hexed:
  'I don't mind my shins,
  Being stuck full of pins,
But I feel I am coming unsexed.'

EDWARD GOREY

The devil's no longer a myth,
But has taken the surname of Smith,
  And become a good sort,
  A sahib, a sport,
A chap we're all intimate with.

LITTLE BILLEE

A psychic researcher's elation
Was shattered by her situation;
  She'd been heard to boast
  That she'd slept with a ghost,
But she now had a phantom gestation.

CYRIL MOUNTJOY

Said an elderly Bishop called Greville,
At a secret episcopal revel:
  'We're distressingly bored
  With the words of the Lord,
So let us discourse on the Devil.'

LITTLE BILLEE

At spirit séances in Queen's,
The spirits make terrible scenes:
   Thus recently Bach
   Shouted angrily: 'Ach!
I'm sick of your damn tambourines!'

MORRIS BISHOP

A man from the *Washington Post*,
Once had it off with a ghost;
   At the height of orgasm,
   The pale ectoplasm
Shrieked: 'Coming! I'm coming . . . almost!'

ANTHONY BURGESS

As played by the phantoms of Shrule,
Midnight football is eerie and cruel;
   If one kicks a ghost
   Past the other's goal-post,
He wins credit for scoring a ghoul.

TONY BUTLER

As tourists inspected the apse,
An ominous series of raps
   Came from under the altar,
   Which caused some to falter,
And others to shriek and collapse.

EDWARD GOREY

As tourists inspected the apse . . .

God's plan made a hopeful beginning,
But Man spoilt his chances by sinning;
　　We trust that the story
　　Will end in great glory,
But at present, the other side's winning.

ANON.

There was an Old Man with a Beard,
Who said: 'I demand to be feared.
　　Address Me as God,
　　And love Me, you sod!'
And Man did just that, which is weird.

ROGER WODDIS

In the Garden of Eden lay Adam
Complacently stroking his madam,
　　And great was his mirth,
　　For he knew that on earth
There were only two balls – and he had 'em.

ANON.

Finding God's taboos totalitarian,
Eve adopted a pose of 'San Fairy Ann',
　　Ate prohibited fruit,
　　Made her mate follow suit,
And left us all quite postlapsarian.

BASIL RANSOME-DAVIES

Each night father fills me with dread,
When he sits on the foot of my bed;
   I'd not mind that he speaks
   In gibbers and squeaks,
But for seventeen years he's been dead.

EDWARD GOREY

The Devil, who plays a deep part,
Has tricked his way into your heart,
   By simple insistence
   On his non-existence
Which really is devilish smart.

LITTLE BILLEE

God brought perfect man to fruition,
But viewing the scraps with contrition,
   He collected the junk,
   And created the skunk,
The snake and the first politician.

DOUGLAS CATLEY

An old archaeologist, Throstle,
Discovered a marvellous fossil.
   He knew from its bend
   And the knob on its end
'Twas the peter of Paul the Apostle.

ANON.

Goliath was known for ferocity,
An expert in every atrocity,
  But was knocked in a heap
  By a boy who kept sheep –
A victim of teenage precocity.

FRANK RICHARDS

Young Joseph's new coat was real nice,
Bright colours and cheap at the price;
  The coat was to take him
  To Egypt and make him
As rich as Lloyd-Webber and Rice.

CYRIL MOUNTJOY

When Jael crept in to see Sisera,
She aimed a bit up from his kisser, her
  Blow, as she said,
  Hit the nail on the head,
And avoided much messier viscera.

BILL GREENWELL

When Lazarus came back from the dead,
He still couldn't function in bed;
  'What good's Resurrection
  Without an erection?'
Old Lazarus testily said.

ANON.

Geography Rules! O.K.?

Throughout the whole world, experts say
That it's GEOGRAPHY RULES! O.K.?
    Though it's not the location
    But the mere appellation
That's important down Limerick way.

There was a young girl of old Natchez,
Whose garments were always in patchez;
   When comment arose
   On the state of her clothes,
She drawled: 'When Ah itchez, Ah scratchez.'

OGDEN NASH

On May Day, the girls of Penzance,
Being bored with the lack of romance,
   Joined the Workers' Parade
   With their banner displayed –
'What the Pants of Penzance need is Ants!'

ANON.

A couturier from Haverford West
Has designed an ankle-length vest;
   She says: 'It's got holes
   For respectable souls
Who can only have sex when they're dressed.'

E. O. PARROTT

There was a young lady from Pecking
Who indulged in a great deal of necking.
   Which seemed such a waste,
   Since she claimed to be chaste –
This statement, however, needs checking.

ANON.

A modest young maiden of Rennes
Would have nothing to do with the mennes,
   But one day at Versailles,
   She was kissed on the slailles,
Now she goes there agennes and agennes.

A.C. COSSINS

There was a young lady of Nantes,
Who lived with a miserly aunt;
   When asked to a ball,
   Said: 'I've no clothes at all.
I must borrow the *plumes* of my *tante.*'

S. LITTMAN

There was a young lady of Nîmes,
Who murdered herself in a dream.
   Since when she repeats
   To all whom she meets:
'I am much more defunct than I seem.'

LITTLE BILLEE

There was an old dame of Toulouse,
Who had no reputation to lose;
   When she revelled at night,
   Her friends thought her too tight,
And her enemies thought her too loose.

A. M. SAYERS

There was a young man of Belgrade
Who planned to seduce a fair maid,
   And as it befell,
   He succeeded quite well,
And the maid, like the plan, was well laid.

ISAAC ASIMOV

A naïve young lady of Bude
Had not seen a man in the nude;
   When a lewd fellow showed
   His all in the road,
She did not know *what* to conclude.

C. CHEVALLIER

There was a young lady of Florence
Who for kissing professed great abhorrence;
   But when she'd been kissed,
   And found what she'd missed,
She cried till her tears came in torrents.

ANON.

A carpenter living in Crewe
Who had nothing whatever to do,
   Once assisted a whore
   With the hinge of her door,
But he made her pay for the screw.

E. O. PARROTT

The French are a race among races;
They screw in the funniest places;
   Any orifice handy
   Is considered quite dandy,
And that goes for the one in their faces.

ANON.

A flighty young lady from Loddon
Fell into a pond and got sodden,
   She took off her clothes
   Then powdered her nose,
And went home feeling thoroughly modern.

IDA THURTLE

There was a young lass of Pitlochry,
Whose morals seemed rather a mockery,
   When they found 'neath her bed
   A lover instead
Of the usual item of crockery.

ANON.

A lady there was in Antigua,
Who said to her spouse: 'What a pig you are!'
   He answered: 'My Queen!
   Is it my manner you mean,
Or do you refer to my figua?'

ANON.

Two middle-aged ladies from Fordham
Went out for a walk and it bored 'em;
  As they made their way back,
  A sex maniac
Leapt out from some trees and ignored 'em.

ANON.

There was a young lady of Leicester
Who had an idea which obseicester;
  When she felt in the mood,
  She'd run round in the nude,
And wonder why no-one posseicester.

ALAN CLARK

I once took my girl to Southend,
Intending a loving weekend;
  But imagine the fuss –
  In the room next to us
Was my wife with a gentleman friend.

VERONICA NICOLSON

A young man who lived at Holme Hale
Went to Acle one day to the sale;
  He waved to his mate,
  And discovered too late
That he'd purchased five acres of kale.

IDA THURTLE

A lady on climbing Mount Shasta,
Complained when the mountain grew vaster;
   It wasn't the climb,
   The dirt or the grime,
But the ice on her ass that harassed her.

ANON.

There was a young girl of Siam,
Who said to her love, young Kiam:
   'If you take me, of course,
   You must do it by force,
But, God knows, you are stronger than I am.'

ANON.

A husband who lived in Tiberias,
Once laughed himself nearly delerious;
   He laughed at his wife,
   Who took a sharp knife,
With results that were quite deleterious.

ANON.

A wanton young lady of Wimley
Reproached for not acting primly,
   Answered: 'Heavens above!
   I know sex isn't love,
But it's such an attractive facsimile.'

ANON.

There was a young girl of Trebarwith
Whom a cad in a car went too far with,
   Which disproves a report
   That she wasn't the sort
For going too far in a car with.

R. J. P. HEWISON

So obese is my cousin from Hendon,
She looks elephantine, seen end on;
   What preys most on her mind
   Is her efforts to find
A good deck-chair that she can depend on.

A. H. BAYNES

I once knew a spinster of Staines,
And a spinster that lady remains;
   She's no figure, no looks,
   Neither dances nor cooks –
And, most ghastly of all, she has brains.

PLAIWON

A couple from old Aberystwyth,
United the organs they kissed with;
   They enjoyed this sweet sharing,
   And did nothing more daring,
And she said: 'You're a right one to tryst with.'

STUART WOODS

A Lady who rules Fort Montgomery
Says the wearing of clothes is a mummery;
   She has frequently tea'd in
   The costume of Eden,
Appearing delightfully summery.

MORRIS BISHOP

A girl who was touring Zambesi
Said: 'Attracting the men is quite easy;
   I don't wear any pants,
   And, at every chance,
I stand where it's frightfully breezy.'

ANON.

Said Queen Isabella of Spain;
'I like it now and again;
   But I wish to explain:
   That by 'now and again'
I mean now, and AGAIN and AGAIN.'

ANON.

There was an old maid of Duluth
Who wept when she thought of her youth,
   And the glorious chances
   She'd missed at school dances,
And once in a telephone booth.

ANON.

Henley's a special regatta,
Where the 'gels' have their annual natter,
  And puce-faced old chaps
  Wear striped blazers and caps,
And the rowing just doesn't matter.

JIM ANTHONY

Said the boy driving home towards Clere:
'We've just run out of petrol, my dear.'
  Said the girl: 'Not to worry!
  I'm not in a hurry.
You get out and push, and I'll steer.'

IDA THURTLE

There was an old housewife of Staines,
Who complained to a man of the drains.
  The council man spat:
  'I've removed the dead cat.
Now it's only the smell that remains.'

E. O. PARROTT

There once was a person of Chiswick,
Who said: 'I despise metaphysic.
  Oxford may feel
  That the real is ideal,
But it certainly isn't in Chiswick.'

J. M. ROSS

There was a young lady of Spain
Who was terribly sick in a train,
   Not once, but again
   And again and again –
And again and again and again.

ANON.

There was a young lady of Chiswick,
Who consulted a Doctor of Physic;
   He tested her hormones,
   And sexual performones,
Then prescribed her a strong aphrodisic.

ANON.

There was a young lady of Aenos,
Who came to our party as Venus;
   We told her: 'How rude
   To come in the nude!'
But we brought her a leaf from the green'ouse.

ANON.

There was a young maiden from Multerry
Whose knowledge of life was desultory;
   She explained, like a sage:
   'Adolescence? The age
Between puberty and – er – adultery.'

ANON.

Said a wife to her husband near Scole,
Who'd forgotten to order the coal:
   'I knew you'd forget.
   You've a head like a net;
Where there isn't a knot there's a hole.'

IDA THURTLE

There was a young girl of Bahari,
Who was chased on a night that was starry;
   She was chased, so she raced,
   Tore her gown in her haste,
And cried: 'I really must go – sew sari!'

R. P. M. LEHMANN

There was a young girl of Tralee,
Whose knowledge of French was '*Oui, oui.*'
   When they said: '*Parlez-vous?*'
   She replied: 'Same to you!'
She was famed for her bright repartee.

ANON.

A poet from Cheltenham Spa,
Had a breakdown whilst driving his car;
   As he scribbled a sonnet,
   Said his bird, 'neath the bonnet:
'You take women's lib much too far.'

BETTY MORRIS

There was a young maid of Peru,
Who swore she never would screw,
    Except under stress
    Of forceful duress,
Like: 'I'm ready. How about you?'

ISAAC ASIMOV

There was a young girl of Penzance,
Who decided to take just one chance;
    She let herself go
    On the lap of her beau,
And now all her sisters are aunts.

ANON.

A youth and a maiden from Costessey,
Sat and talked on a bank that was mostessey;
    After six hours of this,
    The youth ventured a kiss –
Not exactly a speed-merchant, wostessey?

S. C. TURNER

A lama of Outer Mongolia
Was seized by acute melancholia;
    When the Chinese asked why,
    He could only reply:
'You'd chop off my head if I tolia.'

OGDEN NASH

'Active balls?' said an old man of Stoneham:
'I regret that I no longer own 'em.
   But I hasten to say
   They were good in their day –
De mortuis nil nisi bonum.'

C.D.CUDMORE

There was an old person of Persia,
Who called two nasturtiums 'nasturtia'.
   How precious! What pedantry!
   A Pedant and sedentary –
He died of progressive inertia.

WILLIAM PLOMER

There was an old lady of Harrow,
Whose views were exceedingly narrow;
   At the end of her paths,
   She built two bird baths –
For the different sexes of sparrow.

ANON.

A gay soccer spectator from Wix
Thought rugger might offer new tricks;
   He didn't go much
   For kicking for touch,
But fancied the touching for kicks.

CYRIL MOUNTJOY

A señorita who strolled on the Corso
Displayed quite a lot of her torso,
   A crowd soon collected,
   And no-one objected,
Though some were in favour of more so.

                    ANON.

Great-grandfather at Waterloo
Fought solidly all the day through;
   He slashed and he hacked,
   Through bodies tight-packed,
And managed to reach Platform Two.

            FRANK RICHARDS

A lady from near Rising Sun
Flattened her boy-friend in one,
   Saying: 'Don't worry, kid,
   That's for nothing you did
It's for something I dreamed you had done.'

              OGDEN NASH

Said the newly-weds staying near Kitely,
'We turn out the electric light nightly;
   It's best to embark
   Upon sex in the dark,
The *look* of the thing's so unsightly.'

                   ANON.

Some Lives are So Odd

SOME LIVES ARE SO ODD – you agree?
Well worthy of biography.
   The limerick traces
   Their trials and disgraces –
So different from you and from me.

A business-like harlot named Draper
Once tried an unusual caper;
   What made it so nice
   Was you got it half-price,
If you brought in her ad from the paper.

ANON.

Of my husband I do not ask much,
Just an all mod. and con. little hutch;
   Bank account in my name,
   With cheque book to same,
Plus a small fee for fucking and such.

ANON.

Up the street sex is sold by the piece,
And I wish that foul traffic would cease;
   It's a shame and improper,
   And I'd phone for a copper,
But that's where you'll find the police.

ANON.

There was an old madam called Rainey,
Adept at her business, and brainy;
   She charged ten bucks or more,
   For a seasoned old whore,
But a dollar would get you a trainee.

ANON.

When he raped a young maid in a train,
They arrested a fellow named Blaine;
    But the ex-virgin cried:
    'That's for me to decide,
And I'd be the last to complain.'

ANON.

There was a young girl from a Mission,
Who was seized by an awful suspicion,
    That original sin
    Didn't matter a pin
In an era of nuclear fission.

A. H. BAYNES

There was a young girl called Bianca,
Who slept while her ship lay at anchor;
    She awoke with dismay,
    When she heard the mate say:
'Hi! Hoist up the top sheet and spanker!'

ANON.

A vain old Professor of Greek
Would boast: 'I am surely unique.
    The rude *hoi-polloi*
    All cause me no joy.'
So he formed himself into a clique.

RON RUBIN

As the elevator car left our floor,
Big Sue caught her teats in the door;
    She yelled a good deal,
    But had they been real,
She'd have yelled considerably more.

ANON.

After lunch the old Duchess of Teck
Observed: 'If you'll listen one sec.,
    We've found a man's tool
    In the small swimming pool,
So would all of you gentlemen check?'

ANON.

A lonely old maid named Loretta
Sent herself an anonymous letter,
    Quoting Ellis on sex,
    And *Oedipus Rex*,
And exclaimed: 'I already feel better.'

ANON.

There's a very prim girl called McDrood;
What a combo – both nympho and prude!
    She wears her dark glasses
    When fellows make passes,
And keeps her eyes shut when she's screwed.

ANON.

There was a young fellow called Crouch,
Who was courting a girl on a couch;
   She said: 'Why not a sofa?'
   And he exclaimed: 'Oh, for
Christ's sake shut your mouth while I – ouch!'
VICTOR GRAY

An insurance salesman named Flint,
Said with a satisfied squint:
   'Don't try to collect –
   You ought to have checked.
I excluded that clause IN SMALL PRINT.'
CHARLES BARSOTTI

When the census man called upon Gail,
Whose clients were all strictly male,
   And said: 'Your career
   Should be written here.'
She entered the one word: 'Wholesale'.
GEORGE MCWILLIAM

A remarkable race are the Persians;
They have such peculiar diversions.
   They make love all the day
   In the usual way,
And save all the night for perversions.
ANON.

When a friend told a typist called Eve:
'Your boss is too good to believe.
    You can't type, you can't spell.
    Why's he pay you so well?'
She answered: 'I cannot conceive.'

GORDON HARPER

Few people could hope to compare
With the two who made love on the stair.
    When the bannister broke,
    They thought it a joke,
And just carried on in mid-air.

J. ENDERSBY

'Oh, halt!' cried Virginia, 'Enough!
It's not that your beard is too rough.
    Indeed, it's benign –
    So close up to mine,
But why not attempt the real stuff?'

OTTO WATTEAU

We've got a new maid called Chrysanthemum
Who said: 'I have just come from Grantham, mum.
    I lost my last place
    In the sorest disgrace,
'Cos I snored through the National Anthem, mum.'

ANON.

There was an old mickey called Cassidy,
Who was noted for impromptu mendacity.
  When asked did he lie,
  He replied: to reply
Would be to impugn his veracity.

CONRAD AIKEN

A lissom psychotic named Jane
Once kissed every man on a train;
  Said she: 'Please don't panic!
  I'm just nymphomanic.
It wouldn't be fun were I sane.'

ANON.

'On the beach,' said John sadly, 'there's such
A thing as revealing too much.'
  So he closed both his eyes
  At the ranks of bare thighs,
And felt his way through them by touch.

ISAAC ASIMOV

A prudish old lady called Muir
Had a mind so incredibly pure
  That she fainted away
  At a friend's house one day
At the sight of a canary's manure.

ANON.

Undressing a maiden called Sue,
Her seducer exclaimed: 'If it's true
  That a nipple a day
  Keeps the doctor away,
Think how healthy you must be with two.'
BRIAN ALLGAR

There was a young lady called Clarice
Who lived in the city of Paris;
  She wandered with Sartre
  The streets of Montmartre,
But married a chap called Bert Harris.
H.A.C.EVANS

Wanting children a couple once sat
For a course on how to begat.
  When the doctor expounded,
  They stood up dumbfounded,
And said they could never do *that*.
G.W.HANNEY

An old Indian chief, Running B'ar,
At making it rain was a star;
  Asked: 'How do you do it?'
  He replied: 'Nothing to it:
To make rain, me just washum car.'
MARY RITA HURLEY

There was an old Welshman called Morgan
Who had a magnificent organ,
   Said his wife: 'You are blessed
   With what is the best
Hammond organ in all of Glamorgan.'

RON RUBIN

When the judge with his wife having sport
Proved suddenly two inches short,
   The good lady declined,
   And the judge had her fined
By proving contempt of his court.

ANON.

Ethnologists up with the Sioux
Wired home for 'two punts, one canoe'.
   The answer next day
   Said: 'Girls on the way,
But what in hell's name's a 'panoe'?'

ANON.

A lad of the brainier kind
Had erogenous zones in the mind.
   He liked the sensations
   Of solving equations.
(Of course in the end he went blind.)

HYMIE SNEAK

A Texan Rhodes Scholar named Fred
Was a witty companion in bed.
　With priapic zest
　He would toss off each jest.
'I am standing for Congress,' he said.

LYNDON T. MOLE

A left-wing young lady from Wick
Was attacking a Montmartre *flic*.
　When he smacked her behind,
　She observed: 'But how kind!
You're so Gallic and phallic and *chic*.'

GERRY HAMILL

Dad waited while Mum bought the ham.
But when she came out, she said: 'Sam!
　That one's not our baby!'
　He answered: 'Well, maybe,
But look! it's a much nicer pram.'

CORAL E. COPPING

To avoid matrimonial disasters,
Young couples buy Johnson and Masters,
　But trying new angles,
　They get in such tangles,
They end up in splints and in plasters.

MARTIN FAGG

A careless old cook of Salt Ash,
With a second-hand car, had a crash;
   She ploughed through a wall,
   House, garden and all,
And ended up banger and mash.

ANON.

Sighed a dear little shipboard divinity:
'In a deckchair I lost my virginity.
   I was looking to leeward,
   When along came a steward,
And undid my belief in the Trinity.'

CONRAD AIKEN

There was a young lady called Kate,
Who necked in the dark with her date;
   When asked how she fared,
   She said she was scared,
But otherwise doing first-rate.

ANON.

A bottle of perfume that Willie sent
Was highly displeasing to Millicent;
   Her thanks were so cold,
   That they quarrelled, I'm told,
Over that silly scent Willie sent Millicent.

ANON.

As he filled up his order book pp.,
He declared: 'I want higher ww.'
   So he struck for more pay,
   But, alas, they now say
He is sweeping out elephants' cc.

ANON.

The Kings of Peru were the Incas,
Who were known far and wide as great drincas;
   They worshipped the sun,
   And had lots of fun,
But the people all thought them great stincas.

ANON.

It seems I impregnated Marge,
So I do rather feel, by and large,
   Some dough should be tendered
   For services rendered,
But I can't quite decide what to charge.

ANON.

A cute secretary, none cuter,
Was replaced by a clicking computer;
   'Twas the wife of the boss
   Put this deal across,
You see, the computer was neuter.

OGDEN NASH

Said a diffident lady named Drood,
The first time she saw a man nude:
  'I'm glad I'm the sex
  That's concave, not convex –
For I *don't* fancy things that protrude.'

ANON.

The orgy was held on the lawn,
And we knocked off two hours before dawn.
  We found ourselves viewing
  Twenty-two couples screwing,
But by sun-up they'd all come and gone.

ANON.

It occurred when she crossed the Atlantic,
But the screw made young Mamie half frantic;
  It wasn't losing her cherry
  That upset her – not very,
But the aisle of a plane's *not romantic*.

ANON.

On an outing with seventeen Czechs,
A girl tourist supplied the free sex.
  She returned from the jaunt
  Feeling more or less gaunt,
But the Czechs were all absolute wrecks.

ANON.

There was a young lady named Kent,
Who gave up her husband for Lent.
　　The night before Easter,
　　When Jesus released her,
It didn't make a damned bit of difference
because in the meantime he'd been running
around with a whole lot of other women.

ANON.

To her gardener, a lady named Liliom,
Said: 'Billy, plant roses and trilium.'
　　Then started to fool
　　With the gardener's tool,
And wound up in the bed of Sweet William.

ANON.

When Daddy and Mum got quite plastered,
And their shame had been thoroughly mastered,
　　They told their boy, Harry:
　　'Son, we never *did* marry.
But don't tell the neighbours, you bastard.'

ANON.

Said Miss Farrow, on one of her larks:
'Sex is more fun in bed than in parks.
　　You feel more at ease,
　　Your ass doesn't freeze,
And passers-by don't make remarks.'

ANON.

A highly bored damsel called Brown,
Remarked as she laid herself down:
　'I hate to be doing
　This promiscuous screwing,
But what else can you *do* in this town?'

ANON.

Though his plan, when he gave her a buzz,
Was to do what man normally does,
　She declared: 'I'm a Soul,
　Not a sexual goal – '
So he shrugged, and called someone who was.

ANON.

The enjoyment of sex, although great,
Is in later years said to abate.
　This well may be so,
　But how would I know?
I'm now only seventy-eight.

ANON.

There was a young student called Jones,
Who'd reduce any maiden to moans,
　By his wonderful knowledge,
　Acquired in college
Of nineteen erogenous zones.

ANON.

A lisping young lady called Beth
Was saved from a fate worse than death
   Seven times in a row,
   Which unsettled her so,
That she stopped saying 'No' and said 'Yeth.'

ANON.

The Chief Stewardess on a Boeing
When asked where the aircraft was going,
   Said: 'Our navigator
   Is joining us lator.
And till then, we have no way of knowing.'

PAUL ALEXANDER

To his wife said the lynx-eyed detective:
'Can it be that my eyesight's defective?
   Has your west tit the least bit
   The best of your east tit,
Or is it a trick of perspective?'

LANGFORD REED

On Saturn the sexes are three,
A nuisance, I think you'll agree.
   For performing *con brio*,
   You must have a trio,
While it even takes two for a pee.

ANON.

A young girl who was no good at tennis
But at swimming was really a menace,
    Took pains to explain:
    'It depends how you train:
I was a street-walker in Venice.'

                                        ANON.

There was a young Jap on a syndicate,
Who refused his opinions to vindicate;
    He stoutly denied
    That his statements implied
What they seemed on the surface to indicate.

                                        ANON.

'I wouldn't be bothered with drawers,'
Says one of our better-known whawers.
    'There isn't a doubt
    I'm better without,
In handling my everyday chawers.'

                                        ANON.

A young couple who lived at 'The Laurels'
Had the most *indescribable* morals.
    You'd not see in a zoo
    The things that they'd do,
To make up when they had lovers' quarrels.

                          W. F. N. WATSON

Said a luscious young lady called Wade,
On a beach with her charms all displayed:
  'It's so hot in the sun,
  Perhaps rape would be fun,
At least that would give me some shade.'

ANON.

There was a rash fellow called Weir,
Who hadn't an atom of fear;
  He indulged a desire
  To touch a live wire –
And any last line will do here.

ANON.

Said a maid: 'I will marry for lucre.'
And her scandalized ma almost shucre;
  But when the chance came,
  And she told the old dame,
I notice she didn't rebucre.

ANON.

There were once two young people of taste,
Who were beautiful down to the waist;
  So they limited love
  To the regions above,
And so remained perfectly chaste.

MONICA CURTIS

A famed big-hitter in cricket
Slammed his on-drive into a thicket,
   Where girls tanned in the nude,
   And no gent would intrude,
But long-on was on a good wicket.

DOUGLAS CATLEY

A rascal far gone in treachery,
Lured maids to their doom with his lechery;
   He invited them in
   For the purpose of sin,
Though he said 'twas to look at his etchery.

ANON.

An industrious young obstetrician
Conceived his financial position
   To depend upon beauty
   And husbandly duty,
And determined and endless coition.

ISAAC ASIMOV

A sensitive girl called O'Neill
Went on the fairground Big Wheel;
   When half-way around,
   She looked down at the ground,
And it cost her a two-dollar meal.

ANON.

The Natural World

From the west to the fabulous east
Lies THE NATURAL WORLD – used to, at least;
   Look in forest or den,
   In zoo, farm or pen,
Now it's Man that is really the beast.

Consider the lowering Lynx,
He's savage, and sullen, and stynx;
   Though he never has stunk,
   Like the scandalous Skunk –
'Tis a task far beyond him, methinks.

LANGFORD REED

I was thrilled when I went to the Zoo –
They allowed me to bugger the gnu.
   An F. R. Z. S.
   Remarked to me, 'Yes,
It's a privilege granted to few.'

VICTOR GRAY

A slow-footed stockman called Beales
Slipped up with a bull at his heels;
   When trying to rise,
   He got quite a surprise,
Learning something of what a cow feels.

CYRIL MOUNTJOY

There was an old Scot called McTavish,
Who attempted an anthropoid ravish,
   The object of rape
   Was the wrong sex of ape,
And the anthropoid ravished McTavish.

ANON.

There was an old Scot called McTavish . . .

A menagerie came to Cape Race,
Where they loved the gorilla's grimace;
   It surprised them to learn
   He *owned* the concern –
He was human, in spite of his face.

ANON.

I once had a cat called Maria
Who sang like the Huddersfield Choir.
   You could easily know
   She was out with a beau,
For it sounded like Handel's *Messiah*.

PAUL GRIFFIN

A naïve young lady of Cork
Was told she was brought by the stork,
   But after a day
   With a gent called O'Shea,
She was doubtful of that sort of talk.

REG YEARLEY

A shepherd who lived up in Gwent
Kept a dozen old skunks in his tent;
   When asked, 'Do they smell?'
   He answered: 'Too well!
They spotted my scent – so they went.'

E. O. PARROTT

A Professor of Ethical Culture
Once said to his class: "Twould insult your
   Intelligence if
   I said I got stiff
For anything less than a vulture.'

A fellow who fucked but as few can
Had a fancy to try with a toucan.
   He owned like a man
   The collapse of his plan:
'I can't – but I bet none of *you* can!'

As dull as the life of the cloister
(Except it's a little bit moister),
   Mutatis mutandum
   Non est disputandum;
There's no thrill in sex for the oyster.

A creature of charm is the gerbil,
Its diet's exclusively herbal;
   It browses all day
   On great bunches of hay,
And farts with an elegant burble.

There once was a plesiosaurus,
Who lived when the world was all porous;
   But it fainted with shame,
   When it first heard its name,
And departed long ages before us.

ANON.

There was a young woman called Myrtle,
Who once was seduced by a turtle;
   The result of this mate
   Was five crabs and a skate,
Thus proving the turtle was fertile.

ANON.

There was a young man of Wood's Hole,
Who had an affair with a mole;
   He was a bit of a nancy,
   But did like to fancy
Himself in the dominant role.

ANON.

There was a young man of Madras
Who had a magnificent ass;
   Not round and pink,
   As you probably think –
It was grey, had long ears, and ate grass.

ANON.

Two she-camels spied on a goat,
And one jealously said: 'You will note
   She leaves the sheik's tent
   With her tail oddly bent,
And hanks of hair pulled out of her coat.'

ANON.

A southern hill-billy named Hollis,
Used possums and snakes as his solace;
   His children had scales,
   And prehensile tails,
And voted for Governor Wallace.

ANON.

A round-bottomed babe from Mobile
Longed for years to be screwed by a seal,
   But out at the zoo,
   They just said: 'No can do.'
Though the seal is all hot for the deal.

ANON.

Said an eminent, erudite ermine:
'There's one thing I cannot determine:
   When a dame wears my coat,
   She's a person of note –
When I wear it, I'm called only vermin.'

ANON.

Quoth a cow in the marshes of Glynne:
'All the world is divine, even sin.
   As a natural creature,
   I worship all nature,
But most when the bullrush is in.'

CONRAD AIKEN

By Loch Ness they can toss, like confetti,
The proofs that they've snapped, from the jetty,
   Abominable Snowmen?
   Apparently no men
Have ever quite filmed them, as yeti.

BILL GREENWELL

'I'm glad pigs can't fly,' said young Sellers
(He's one of those worrying fellers).
   'For if they could fly,
   They'd shit in the sky,
And we'd all have to carry umbrellas.'

RON RUBIN

Said an ape as he swung by his tail,
To his offspring both female and male:
   'From your offspring, my dears,
   In a couple of years,
May evolve a professor at Yale.'

ANON.

Giraffes, yes, even the strongest,
Hang back in love's headlong conquest;
   They have a motter
   Which says that they gotter:
'He who giraffes last, giraffes longest.'

FRANK DAVIES

A herder who hailed from Terre Haute,
Fell in love with a young nanny-goat;
   The daughter he sired
   Was greatly admired
For her beautiful angora coat.

ANON.

Good mechanics are all of one mind
That a ball-race is rightly defined
   As the miserable plight
   Of a tom-cat in flight
From a vet two paces behind.

DOUGLAS CATLEY

There was an old person of Slough,
Who took all his meals with a cow,
   Always said: 'It's uncanny,
   She's so like Auntie Fanny,'
But he never would indicate how.

GEORGE ROBEY

There was a young peasant named Gorse,
Who fell madly in love with a horse;
  Said his wife: 'You rapscallion,
  The horse is a stallion –
This constitutes grounds for divorce.'

ANON.

Said a dreadfully literate cat:
'I've had my Litt.D. and all that,
  And in New York, my dear,
  When I see "Litter here",
Why I litter at once, and then scat.'

CONRAD AIKEN

A French poodle espied in the hall
A pool that a damp gamp let fall,
  And said: 'Ah, *oui, oui*!
  This time it's not me,
But I'm bound to be blamed for it all.'

ANON.

There once was an eccentric of Metz,
Who filled all his villa with pets,
  Who filled all the floors,
  Both windows and doors,
Which just left an outhouse for vets.

LESLIE JOHNSON

There were three little owls in a wood,
Who sang hymns whenever they could.
  What the words were about,
  One could never make out,
But one felt it was doing them good.

ANON.

A monkey exclaimed with great glee:
'The things in this zoo that I see!
  The curious features
  Of all those strange creatures
That come and throw peanuts at me!'

FRANK RICHARDS

A Fat-tailed Dwarf Lemur, in bed
With the father of hangovers, said:
  'My very large rudder
  Makes most females shudder,
And now I've acquired a fat head.'

GERRY HAMILL

A pushing young man in Patchogue
Runs a Radio Hour for the Dog.
  His programme of growls,
  Barks, bays, whines and howls
Is setting the dog world agog.

MORRIS BISHOP

Airs Grave and Gentle

Sometimes there are AIRS GRAVE AND
    GENTLE,
Religious, or, perhaps, sentimental
    Or the limerick's lyric,
    Or else panegyric,
Or struggles with things elemental.

How often and often I wish
I lived in green depths like a fish!
   No noise. Not a thing,
   But the mermaids who sing,
Whilst their tails give a silvery swish.

FRANCES CORNFORD

Precede us, O Lord, with Thy Grace,
As we travel through Time and through Space,
   In all that we do,
   May we magnify You,
Our reward as we run the straight race.

TRADITIONAL (Version by Frank R. McManus)

There was a Young Lady in White
Who looked out in the depth of the night;
   But the birds of the air
   Filled her with despair
And depressed that Young Lady in White.

EDWARD LEAR

O God, for as much as without Thee
We are not enabled to doubt Thee,
   Help us by Thy Grace
   To convince the whole race,
We know nothing whatever about Thee.

RONALD KNOX

A Fascist, erect and irate,
With the pose of implacable fate,
  Said: 'Our triumph has been
  To make a machine
To be worked by the will of the Great.'
THOMAS THORNELEY

The reason we're asked to endure
A gutter press, smutty, impure,
  Is that old river Fleet,
  Whose name's on the street,
Is an ordurous, underground sewer.
BILL GREENWELL

A Millionaire, filled with elation
At his newspaper's wide circulation,
  Said: 'With murder, divorces,
  And hints about horses,
I am moulding the mind of the nation.'
THOMAS THORNELEY

Said a Tripper: 'O joy, to have found
Such a glory of sight and of sound!
  How our heart-strings are stirred
  By the song of a bird,
As we scatter our litter around!'
THOMAS THORNELEY

[*Night Scene*]

There's a slow tolling bell in the dark
As the keepers are clearing the park.
  Like a desert, it's bare;
  And each tree and each chair
Is a blurred indeterminate mark.

GAVIN EWART

[*Autumn*]

Life is sad and so slow and so cold
As the leaves that were green turn to gold,
  As the lonely lake fills
  And there's ice in the hills
And the long loathly winter takes hold. . .

GAVIN EWART

Concerning the bees and the flowers,
In the fields and the gardens and bowers;
  You will tell at a glance
  That their ways of romance
Haven't any resemblance to ours.

ANON.

Winter is here with his grouch,
The time when you sneeze and you slouch;
  You can't take your women
  Canoein' or swimmin',
But a lot can be done on a couch.

ANON.

Most women get married, 'tis true,
They feel it's the best they can do;
   But why spend your life
   Being somebody's wife,
When you might spend it just being you?

BARNEY BLACKLEY

There was a French bard who said: 'Hell!
This life's a perpetual farewell;
   The new-born's first sigh
   Is a sort of goodbye,
And Death's always ringing the bell.'

TOWANBUCKET

I'm getting deep lines on my forehead;
My face is becoming quite florid.
   I measure with dread
   My middle-aged spread;
I think growing old is quite horrid.

RON RUBIN

[*The Face*]

As a beauty I'm not a great star,
There are others more handsome by far;
   But my face I don't mind it,
   Because I'm behind it,
It's the folks out in front that I jar.

ANTHONY EUWER

As the poets have mournfully sung,
Death takes the innocent young,
  The rolling-in-money,
  The screamingly funny,
And those who are very well hung.

W. H. AUDEN

A one-day-old baby in Wallabout
Reflected: 'Oh, what is it all about?
  I comprehend not
  Whence, whither or what,
But I'm sure it is something to squall about.'

MORRIS BISHOP

The Life-Force, afflicted with doubt,
As to what it was bringing about,
  Cried: 'Alas, I am blind,
  But I'm making a Mind
That may possibly puzzle it out.'

THOMAS THORNELEY

If no Pain were, how judge we of Pleasure?
If no Work, where's the solace of Leisure?
  What's White, if no Black?
  What's Wealth, if no Lack?
If no Loss, how our Gain could we measure?

WILLIAM BLISS

[Australian Wildlife]

There's an emerald frog down the loo;
Please beware of the funnel-web who
   Lies in wait by the door;
    Snakes breed under the floor,
And your supper of shark could eat you.

RUTH SILCOCK

[Every Picture Tells a Story]

In the rain in a yard in Cessnock,
Sits a housewife in hat, gloves and frock;
   Umbrella held high
    To keep her beer dry,
In the yard of the pub at Cessnock.

RUTH SILCOCK

[Flowering Sydney Suburb]

Hibiscus is flaming and frillier;
Oleander is neater and chillier;
   Frangipani smells sweeter,
    But is somehow effeter
Than a tower of puce Bougainvillea.

RUTH SILCOCK

[Drought]

A land of blue skies, and sunlight,
Each day endlessly clear and bright.
   Without rain, the dams dry,
    Crops fail, cattle die,
Farmers waste, walk away, quit the fight.

RUTH SILCOCK

Evangelical Vicar in want
Of a portable second-hand font,
  Would exchange for the same
  A portrait (in frame)
Of the Bishop-Elect of Vermont.

RONALD KNOX

Widow (conscious that time's on the wing),
Fortyish, but still game for a fling,
  Seeks fun-loving male,
  Mature, but not stale,
With a view to the usual thing.

STANLEY J. SHARPLESS

I wish that my room had a floor.
I don't so much care for a door,
  But this crawling around
  Without touching the ground
Is getting to be quite a bore.

GELETT BURGESS

They say that I was in my youth
Uncouth and ungainly, forsooth;
  I can only reply:
  'Tis a lie, 'tis a lie!
I was couth, I was perfectly couth.

ANON.

There's a tiresome young man of Bay Shore.
When his fiancée cried: 'I adore
   The beautiful sea!'
   He replied: 'I agree
It's pretty, but what is it for?'

MORRIS BISHOP

Big cities are reeking with grief;
A haven for rapist and thief,
   And designed in a way
   So that half of us pay
To maintain all the rest on relief.

ANON.

It's time to make love, douse the glim;
The fireflies twinkle and dim;
   The stars lean together
   Like birds of a feather,
And the loin lies down with the limb.

CONRAD AIKEN

There was a young person of Leigh
Who was either a he or a she;
   I think it's terrific
   To be non-specific
Gender-wise, don't you agree?

BASIL RANSOME-DAVIES

If Eve hadn't eaten the apple,
Mankind would have no need to grapple
   With sin and temptation,
   And disapprobation
From ladies who worship at chapel.

WENDY COPE

In Genesis, Adam's the winner,
Whilst Eve is denounced as the sinner
   For the fruit that she brings;
   That's how men see things:
He blames *her* when she brings his dinner.

BILL GREENWELL

Of all God's jokes none is bluer
Than when He mixed sex with manure.
   What was on His Mind
   When He saddled mankind
With a playground alongside a sewer?

A. CINNA

[*La Nausée*]

Angst, poetry, urbanized fret,
Have my *authentique* stomach upset.
   Beauty is horror –
   We'll see no tomorrow –
(It's more than just something I ate!)

SYDNEY BERNARD SMITH

There was a young fellow of Perth,
Who was born on the day of his birth;
    He was married, they say,
    On his wife's wedding day,
And died when he quitted the earth.

ANON.

We've socially-conscious biography,
Aesthetics and social geography;
    Today every field
    Boasts its Marxist yield,
So now we've class-conscious pornography.

ANON.

Lord, since it is hard to explain
By reason, the problem of Pain,
    Assist us to revel
    In talk of the Devil,
And spare us the use of the brain.

JOHN PRESS

[*'The perpetual overdraft is bad for the
community as a whole'* – Speech by Banker]

Since my overdraft threatens to be
Detrimental to sound industry,
    I surrender all claim
    That it stands in my name.
Mr Banker, I trust you'll agree.

S. TONKIN

The Limerick Fringe

Though the limerick can not be deaded,
In THE LIMERICK FRINGE it's beheaded,
  Is double, extended,
  Unrhymed or up-ended,
Or else to the haiku is wedded.

THE DOUBLE LIMERICK

The Limerick issued from Lear,
  The Clerihew blossomed in Bentley;
The former was foolish and queer,
  The latter guyed history gently.
  But they both of them gave,
    On their path to the grave,
  So much pleasure in print,
    That we'd most of us waive
Any critical right to be hard upon Lear
  Or turn up our noses at Bentley.

J. A. LINDON

There was an old Begum of Frome,
  There was an old Yogi of Leicester;
She sent him a tulip in bloom,
  He rolled his black eyes and he blessed her.
  How replete with delight
    Is a flower to the sight;
  It brightens the day,
    And it sweetens the night.
Oh! if all the old ladies grew tulips in Frome,
  How happy the Yogis of Leicester.

WALTER DE LA MARE

That rebellious rodent called Jerry,
    And his chum, the cat-astrophe, Tom,
Have perpetual hatchets to bury
    And get like a hydrogen bomb;
        Whenever the feline
        Is making a bee-line
            For succulent prey
            In his truculent way
He has several bites of the cherry,
    But the mouse chews him up with aplomb.

BILL GREENWELL

A fiery young fellow called Bryant
    Was struck by a maiden called May,
And though he was almost a giant,
    And she but a tiny thing, they
        Were very soon wedded
        For both were hot-headed,
            Her first name was Vesta,
            And once he possessed her
She turned out agreeably pliant,
    And the match has survived to this day.

BARNEY BLACKLEY

There was a young lady named Miller,
    And a similar one called Miss Dors,
Each renowned as a brassière filler,
    They seemed to defy Nature's laws.
    For the actress a 'must'
    Is an oversized bust.
    You may think it's just
    An encitement to lust,
But with it her fate's to go sweeping the States,
    When without she makes more sweeping floors.

                                    AUSTEN BAKER

As he stood in their shop, Mr Boosey,
    Was approached by his partner, one Hawkes,
Saying: 'Please, I don't wish to sound choosey,
    But the whole of the music trade baulks
    At your off-putting surname –
    It's more of a slur-name –
        With gross connotations
        Of beery libations,
Evoking some four-ale bar floozie,
    And the Freudian popping of corks.

                                    JIMMY PEARSE

The first of all people was Adam,
    And out of his ribs appeared Eve;
Her primary task was to pad 'em,
    The pain of her birth to relieve.
She fed him with fruit,
And attempted a suit,
        But God said: 'How crude!
    Though you cease to be nude,
Never hope, my unfortunate madam,
    Your apronless state to retrieve.'

MOIRA BLYTH

[Buttons]

There was an old skinflint of Hitching
    Had a cook, Mrs Casey of Cork,
There was nothing but crusts in the kitchen,
    While the parlour was sherry and pork.
    So at last Mrs Casey, her pangs to assuage,
    Having snipped off his buttons, curried the page.
    And now, while the skinflint gulps sherry and pork,
    In his parlour adjacent to kitchen,
To the tune blithe and merry of knife and of fork,
    Anthropophagy reigns in the kitchen.

WALTER DE LA MARE

THE EXTENDED LIMERICK

There once were two cats of Kilkenny,
Each thought there was one cat too many,
    So they quarrelled and fit,
    They scratched and they bit,
    Till, barring their nails
    And the tips of their tails,
Instead of two cats, there weren't any.

ANON.

There was a strange student from Yale,
Who puts himself outside the pale.
    Said the judge: 'Please refrain
    When passing through Maine,
    From exposing yourself again in the train,
Or you'll just have to do it in jail.'

ANON.

An Opera Teacher neemed Enna
Seng songs in a moost refained menna,
    Though small in the freem,
    She was wade in the beam,
    And her mean soshal eam
    Was to moove out of Cheam,
    For her pewpils all keem
    From the *cream de la cream*.
But she sensed no esteem
From the neeberhood scream:
'Tek yer Barbershop team,
Get the 'ell art'er Cheam,
And accompany them on the pienna!'

MOSS RICH

THE LIMERAIKU

The limeraiku, which was the invention of Ted Pauker, combines the form of the Japanese haiku
(three lines of 5, 7 and 5 syllables),
but also incorporates the rhyming scheme of the limerick.

There's a vile old man
Of Japan who roars at whores:
'Where's your bloody fan?'

TED PAUKER

Little Miss Muffet
Said: 'Stuff it. No go. And so,
Hands off my tuffet.'

W. S. BROWNLEE

Said Little Boy Blue:
'Same to you. You scorn my horn?
You know what to do.'

W. S. BROWNLEE

There was an old pros
From Sri Lanka whose chancre
Grew lichen and moss.

ZELDA CHEVETTE

In Arabia,
Baby, a girl *must* get dust
In her labia.

GERTRUDE GERARD

An old soak from Stoke
Likes tarts to ignite his farts.
You should see the smoke.
C. J. PARKER

There's a cut-price whore
Of Cawnpore who hails all males:
'Bed, Mattress – or Floor?'
PASCOE POLGLAZE

There's a man at Crewe
Station who buggers muggers
So well there's a queue.
E. O. PARROTT

John Keats rose at dawn
Still forlorn, too chaste to taste
The amorous Brawne.
NICK ENRIGHT

There's a latent queer
Of Tangier, who brays at gays:
'I'm hetero, dear.'
TIM HOPKINS

That raddled old queen
Is the Dean. Just scents a gents,
And . . . know what I mean?
TOM DONNELLY

THE REVERSE LIMERICK –
IN REPLY TO VERSES BY EDWARD LEAR

There was an Old Man with a Beard,
Who said: 'It is just as I feared!
   Two Owls and a Hen,
   Four Larks and a Wren,
Have all built their nests in my beard.'

EDWARD LEAR

[*The Replies*]

I've combed out my beard and I've found
   Eggs, woodcocks on toast,
   Birds' nest soup, fowls to roast . . .
In more senses than one, I'll be bound,
It suited me down to the ground.

PAULINE PHILLIPS

My beard's overcrowded. Now that
   I freely admit,
   But why should Lear sit
In judgement? He might find a bat
If he lifted his runcible hat.

RICHARD UNWIN

Dear Sir, You're quite wrong about me.
   No wren or small fowl
   Would nest with an owl,
In one beard – they would never agree.
How very absurd you can be!

M. TRENCH

There was a Young Lady of Portugal
Whose ideas were excessively nautical.
  She climbed up a tree
  Just to look at the sea,
But decided she would never leave Portugal.

EDWARD LEAR

[*The Reply*]

No Portuguese Lady is Nautical
  I became a tree–climber
  To escape from a rhymer
Whose conduct was highly cavortical,
And whose leer was too *Vive-le-Sportical*.

SIDNEY HOFFMAN

There was an Old Man on some rocks,
Who shut his wife up in a box;
  When she said: 'Let me out!'
  He exclaimed: 'Without doubt,
You will pass all your life in that box.'

EDWARD LEAR

[*The Reply*]

My purpose was purely corrective
  But the lid that you drew
  Would never close to,
Which rendered my scheme ineffective
How I wish you had studied perspective.

LESLIE JOHNSON

There was a Young Lady of Portugal . . .

There was an Old Person of Basing,
Whose presence of mind was amazing;
*   He purchased a steed,*
*   Which he rode at full speed,*
And escaped from the people of Basing.

EDWARD LEAR

[*The Replies*]

I admire your felicitous phrasing,
    Though you fail to record
    That I flourished a sword
To intimidate crowds that were gazing
In disgust at my exit from Basing.

A. M. SAYERS

Don't thee think, Zurrr, I be zo amazin'
    If ever thee's spoke
    With one of this folk
Thee'd have quit this daft 'amlet of Basin'
Fast as if all thine ricks be'd a-blazin'.

ELIZABETH H. LISTER

Who, or why, or which, or what is the Akond of Swat?
  Is he tall or short,
    Or dark or fair?
Does he sit on a stool or sofa or chair, or squat,
The Akond of Swat?

EDWARD LEAR

[*The Akond of Swat Strikes Back*]

Mr Lear, I'm the Akond of Swat.
  I'm gracious and fat,
    In a very tall hat,
And I'm heating a very large pot.
You know, and for whom, and for what.

ETHEL TALBOT SCHEFFAUER

I fear, Mr Lear, you're a clot.
  You *may* ask, Who is Noah?
    Or George Bernard Shaw?
Or Beethoven? Or Sir Walter Scott?
But NEVER the Akond of Swat!

ERIC SWAINSON

THE BEHEADED LIMERICK

A nice pot of gold that was mari,
Belonged to a dan that was harri
   When some cals who were ras
   Filled their kets which were bas
She put up a cade which was barri.

ARTHUR SHAW

A certain young pate who was addle
Rode a horse he alleged to be saddle,
   But his gust which was dis,
   For his haps which were mis,
Sent him back to his lac which was Cadil.

ARTHUR SHAW

In gonia once which was Pata,
A clysm occurred which was cata.
   A gineer that was en
   Lost his ture that was den,
In a torium there that was nata.

ARTHUR SHAW

A chap was so pose that was adi
And the butt of such nage that was badi.
   He solved that was re
   Not to lay that was de
In taking steps cal that were radi.

ARTHUR SHAW

THE TONGUE-TWISTER

A tutor who tooted a flute
Tried to teach two young tooters to toot.
   Said the two to the tutor:
   'Is it harder to toot, or
To tutor two tooters to toot?'

CAROLYN WELLS

A certain young chap named Bill Beebee,
Was in love with a lady named Phoebe;
   'But,' he said, 'I must see
   What the clerical fee
Be before Phoebe be Phoebe Beebee.'

ANON.

A flea and a fly in a flue
Were imprisoned, so what could they do?
   Said the fly: 'Let us flee'
   Said the flea: 'Let us fly!'
So they flew through a flaw in the flue.

ANON.

A canner, exceedingly canny,
One morning remarked to his granny:
   'A canner can can
   Anything that he can,
But a canner can't can a can, can he?'

CAROLYN WELLS

There was a young person called Tate,
Who went out to dine at 8.08;
   But I will not relate
   What that person named Tate
And his tête-à-tête ate at 8.08.

CAROLYN WELLS

A keeper who worked at the zoo,
Received a new gnu to see to.
   He said: 'That's the gnu
   That I knew at Bellevue –
I knew that I knew that new gnu.'

FRANK RICHARDS

A traveller to Timbuktu
Said: 'Pilot! It's time that we flew!'
   He replied: 'That will do!
   Your watch is askew:
It's a minute or two to 2.02.'

ANON.

THE YOUNG GIRL FROM UTTOXETER

I'm in love with a girl from Uttoxeter,
An exquisite and passionate cock-sitter;
   With her prehensile hole,
   She envelopes my pole,
And then squirms up and down as my rocks hit her.

GERARD BENSON

A horsewoman of charm at Uttoxeter
Caused a scene with much shaking of locks at her;
   When announcing 'Hunt Cup',
   The P. A. mixed it up,
And began a stampede by the Jocks at her.

R. D. CONDON

There was a young girl from Uttoxeter,
Who sported a tight-fitting baroque sweater;
   Her mother cried: 'Smart?
   You look like a tart.'
And flung accusations of pox at her.

STANLEY J. SHARPLESS

There was a young girl of Uttoxeter,
Who worked nine to five as a choc-setter;
   She rolled the chocs thin
   With a wee rolling-pin,
So they'd fit in the After Eight box better.

STANLEY J. SHARPLESS

A teacher of tots at Uttoxeter
Who chucked their constructional blocks at her,
  Was thinking: 'Aggression
  Is just self-expression',
When a volley of paperback Spocks hit her.

KATE MCPOWER

There was a young girl of Uttoxeter
Who noticed that men waved their cocks at her;
  This would cause some surprises
  In nearby Devizes,
But it's what they all do in Uttoxeter.

D. KARTUN

There was a young girl from Uttoxeter
Who one dreary night had a fox at her;
  She let out a squeal,
  For his cock was like steel,
But she had quite a shock when the pox hit her.

GEORGE COWLEY

There was a young girl from Uttoxeter,
Who out on a date with two Jocks at a
  Disco in Wick,
  Slipped off with a Mick –
No wonder those two Jocks threw rocks at her.

BOB SCOTT

There was a young girl from Uttoxeter
Who kept hens, but refused to have cocks. It a-
  Rose from her youth,
  When some rather uncouth
Farm-hands raised up their smocks at her.

ALASTAIR CHAMBRE

There was a young girl from Uttoxeter,
Who made passing oarsmen gape through locks at her.
  At their annual ball,
  They agreed one and all,
They would craftily point their small cox at her.

L. W. BAILEY

She was caught, a young girl of Uttoxeter
In flagrante delicto, two Jocks at her,
  As the customers came,
  Cameras clicked (to their shame)
And the photos were captioned 'Two-Cock Satyr'.

TIM HOPKINS

A kinky young girl from Uttoxeter
Adored having men wave their socks at her;
  She was cleaned of this stain
  By a priest from Dunblane
Who quoted St Paul and John Knox at her.

HERBERT KRETZMER

HAPPY RELATIONS

There's a wonderful family called Stein:
There's Gert and there's Ep and there's Ein.
  Gert's poems are bunk,
  Ep's statues are junk,
And no-one can understand Ein.

ANON.

Three wonderful people called Ley;
There's Hen and there's Bench and there's Hea.
  Hen wrote jingoistic verse,
  Bench wrote *Jaws*, which is worse,
And the less said the better of Hea.

TIM HOPKINS

Each Lon was a notable man:
Greek So, French Vil and Brit Scan,
  So made people think,
  Vil was put in the clink,
And the plebs made a Lord out of Scan.

L.G.UDALL

The Sky's are a pitiful lot,
There's Chom and there's Spas and there's Trot.
  Trot chose the wrong lobby,
  Spas flunked out to Bobby,
And the structures of Chom are all rot.

BOB SCOTT

Three Aldis, not one of them dim,
Were Garib and Frescob and Grim.
   One played and one clowned
   And the other's renowned
By a biscuit that's named after him.

JOYCE JOHNSON

Three wonderful people called Wick:
There's War and there's Chad and there's Pick.
   War said: 'Kings, come on!'
   Chad found the neutron,
And all the world knows Mr Pick.

A. M. SAYERS

Three scribblers whose names end in Bert
Gil, Her and Flau – are now inert.
   Gil wrote silly songs,
   Her satirized wrongs
And Flau was once set for School Cert.

C. VITA-FINZI

How varied the family Sen!
For instance, Sun Yat, Ib and Jen
   Sun Yat changed Cathay,
   Ib wrote play after play,
And Jen played and changed the Top Ten.

ROY FULLER

THE YOUNG LADY OF ULVA

There was a wee lassie of Ulva
Who was blessed with a rather guid vulva.
  For a fiver she'd say,
  You can ha' me all day,
If you've no notes, I'll make do wi' sulva.

DAVID FISHER

There was a young lady from Ulva,
Whose music-hall turn with a culver
  Evoked great applause,
  As she tore off her drawers,
And induced it to swoop up her vulva.

RUSSELL LUCAS

There was a young lady of Ulva
Who said: 'I have granted a culver,
  One fox and a vole,
  Two mice and a mole,
A refuge from Man in my vulva.'

T. GRIFFITHS

There was a young lady of Ulva
Whose boy-friend said: 'Look, I will pulver-
  ize any of you blokes
  Who try to make blue jokes
Concerning my Ulva girl's vulva.'

STANLEY J. SHARPLESS

There was a young lady of Ulva
Who was famed far and wide for her vulva;
  Most Englishmen said
  It was herrings and bread –
But the Turks said it tasted of halva.
                              GAVIN EWART

There was a young lady of Ulva,
Whose sexual feelings were null. Va-
  ginal climaxes
  Came as rarely as taxis,
And she'd nothing but void in her vulva.
                              BARBARA E. GOFF

There was a young lady of Ulva
Who drunkenly said: 'What a hulva
  Party ya mizd,
  Why I gozzo pizd
I saw more lil' people than Gulva.'
                              BILL GREENWELL

There was a young lady of Ulva
Who kept a pet bee in her hand-bag.
  Her lover, called Jock,
  Was stung on the arm,
So to soothe him she bought him a box of best Turkish delight.
                              T. JOHNSTON

THE LIMICK

An old person of Troy
In the bath is so coy
That it doesn't know yet
If it's a girl or a boy.

OGDEN NASH

Two nudists of Dover,
When purple all over,
Were munched by a cow,
When mistaken for clover.

OGDEN NASH

A young flirt of Ceylon,
Who led the boys on,
Playing 'Follow the Leda',
Succumbed to a swan.

OGDEN NASH

A cook called McMurray
Got a raise in a hurry
From his Hindu employer,
By flavouring curry.

OGDEN NASH

THE LIMERICK POEM

[*The Old Man of Nantucket*]

There was an Old Man of Nantucket,
Who kept all his cash in a bucket.
 His daughter, called Nan,
 Ran away with a man,
And as for the bucket, Nantucket.

Pa followed the pair to Pawtucket
(The man and the girl with the bucket)
 And he said to the man:
 'You're welcome to Nan!'
But as for the bucket, Pawtucket.

Then the pair followed Pa to Mannhasset,
Where he still held the cash as an asset;
 And Nan and the man
 Stole the money and ran,
And as for the bucket, Mannhasset.

ANON.

[*Prevalent Poetry*]

A wandering tribe called the Siouxs,
Wore moccasins, having no shiouxs.
 They are made of buckskin,
 With fleshy side in,
Embroidered with beads of bright hiouxs.

When out on the war-path the Siouxs
March single-file – never by tiouxs,
   And by 'blazing' the trees,
   Can return at their ease,
And their way through the forest ne'er liouxs.

All new-fangled boats he eschiouxs,
And uses the birch-bark caniouxs,
   These are handy and light,
   And, inverted at night,
Give shelter from storms and from diouxs.

The principal food of the Siouxs
Is Indian maize which they briouxs,
   And hominy make,
   Or mix in a cake,
And eat it with pork as they chiouxs.

Now doesn't this spelling look ciouxrious?
'Tis enough to make anyone fiouxrious.
   So a word to the wise!
   Pray our language revise,
With orthography not so injiouxrious.

CHARLES FOLLEN ADAMS

[Pioneer Village]

This is Pioneer Village. The sun
Bakes a field of log-houses to dun.
   Each historical hut
   Is boarded up, shut.
We shout, shake the gates, wake no-one.

So we climb the fence, trespass, explore.
There's a court-house, a schoolroom, a store,
   Barns of furniture, sheds,
   Stacked with carts, double beds.
Freezers, motor-bikes, prams cram the floor.

We poke about, ponder this place.
Someone's missing. We call, rush and chase,
   Search an outhouse, a shack.
   Here she is, coming back,
A parasol shading her face.

We squint at the school through a chink.
Yellow maps, lesson books, blackened ink.
   We can just see the date.
   Nineteen fifty-eight.
Museums for the living, we think.

RUTH SILCOCK

[Heredity]

The primitive Pithecanthropus erectus,
With whom the ethnologists rightly connect us,
   Defended his own
   By cudgel and stone,
Why isn't our ancestor here to protect us?

The arrogant Pithecanthropus erectus,
Whose traits, through inheritance, deeply affect us,
   Was sure it was good
   To grab all he could,
Like some of his offspring whose morals deject us.

The ape-man, Pithecanthropus erectus,
Has many descendants prepared to dissect us,
   With them might is right,
   And if we can't fight,
There's nothing at all will make them respect us.

ARTHUR GUITERMAN

[*Summary*]

(Written at the age of thirteen and a half as a 'prep' exercise)

Whatever will rhyme with Summer?
There only is 'plumber' and 'drummer':
   Why! the cleverest bard
   Would find it quite hard
To connect with the Summer – a plumber!

My Mind's getting glummer and glummer
Hooray! there's a word besides drummer;
   Oh, I will think of some
   Ere the prep's end has come
But the rhymes will get rummer and rummer.

Ah! If the bee hums, it's a hummer;
And the bee showeth signs of the Summer;
   Also holiday babels
   Make th'porter gum labels,
And whenever he gums, he's a gummer!

The cuckoo's a goer and comer
He goes in the hot days of Summer;
   But he cucks ev'ry day
   Till you plead and you pray
That his voice will get dumber and dumber!

SIR JOHN BETJEMAN

[*The Deadly Seven*]

In Ireland, we're all of us just –
Seven deadlies? You think we're that fussed?
   There's one of the seven
   Will bar you from Heaven –
North or South – it's anathema – Lust.

We've inverted the rest (aren't we snide?)
And partitioned them out, three a side,
   So the Northerner's claim
   To a virtuous name
Rests on Covetous Anger and Pride

While the Southerners swear, little loth –
Economic and spiritual growth
   May be part of the story,
   But where lies true glory?
In Gluttony, Envy and Sloth.

SYDNEY BERNARD SMITH

[*Ratatouille*]

This *plat* is a true Ratatouille;
And who says French cooking is hooey?
   It still has the edge
   On *Angleterre*'s vedge:
Ha, ha! *et à bas le chou bouilli!*

So sweat your courgettes till they're dewy
(For *l'eau* is the foe of *celui*)
   While, golden in *huile*,
   As tomatoes you peel,
Your chopped onions fry free of *ennui*.

Red peppers and aubergines bluey
You stew *in fragrantio sui*,
   And add a last sigh
   Of *estragon* and *ail*
As you lie on the floor with the Pouilly . . .

Mais qu'est-ce c'est que ce bruit?
Le reste du repas n'est pas cu-it –
   But the guests on the mat
   At the door of your flat
Go *ratatatatatatouille!*

GINA BERKELEY

THE UNRHYMED LIMERICK

There was an old fellow called Hugger,
Who was captain and mate of a fishing smack;
   When a yacht crossed his bows,
   He said: 'My word!
It's an awfully good thing it wasn't a liner.'

ARNOLD HYDE

An American girl in Versailles
Said: 'I feel so ashamed I could weep.
   Ten days I've been here
   And not gone to the Louvre.'
'Never mind,' said someone, 'it's probably only the hard water.'

C.K.B.

There was a young lady of Ealing
Who walked up and down on the window;
   And there, for a while,
   To vary her technique,
She practised strathspeying and hornpipes.

ALLEN M. LAING

There was a young lady called Dawes,
Went out to a dance without gloves;
   Her ma said: 'Amelia!
   Should anyone dance with you,
He'll take you for one of them actresses.'

ANON.

Revelations

REVELATIONS – we've come to the lewd,
The risqué, the bawdy, the rude,
   And all those narrations
   Of sex aberrations
I'm certain you all have eschewed.

[Auto-Erotic]

You'll never know *how* good you are
Till you try to make love in a car.
  Many a man meets defeat
  On a darkened back seat,
It's only the experts break par.

                    ANON.

A young bride and groom of Australia
Remarked as they joined genitalia:
  'Though the system seems odd,
  We are thankful that God
Developed the genus *Mammalia*.'

                    ANON.

Connoisseurs of coition aver
That young British ladies don't stir.
  This condition, in Persia
  Is known as inertia,
And it's *not* the response I prefer.

                    ANON.

On a date with a charming young bird,
His erotical feelings were stirred;
  So with bold virile pluck,
  He inquired: 'Do you fuck?'
She said: 'Yes, but don't use that word.'

                    ANON.

'Well, I took your advice, Doc,' said Knopp,
'Told my wife she'd like it on top.
   She bounced for an hour,
   Till she ran out of power,
And the kids, who got bored, made her stop.'

ANON.

Come and see our French goods – you can try 'em,
Fit them on for right size when you buy 'em:
   Strong, smooth, and reversible,
   The thinnest dispersible;
Any *odd* shape you need, we supply 'em.

ANON.

Try our Rubber Girl-Friend (air-inflatable),
Perennially young (quite insatiable).
   Our satisfied clients,
   From mere midgets to giants,
Say she's incredibly sexy and mateable.

ANON.

None could better our sex limousine,
With its neat, built-in Fucking Machine:
   Engine-powered, this connects
   To suit either sex,
And adjusts to the fat and the lean.

ANON.

There once was a monarch of Spain,
Who was terribly naughty and vain;
   When women were nigh,
   He would open his fly,
And have them with sneers of disdain.

ANON.

There was a young fellow called Wyatt,
Who had a big girl on the quiet,
   But down on the wharf,
   He kept a nice dwarf,
Just in case he should go on a diet.

ANON.

There was a young fellow called Lancelot,
Whom his neighbours all looked on askance a lot;
   Whenever he'd pass
   A presentable lass,
The front of his pants would advance a lot.

ANON.

Said the mythical King of Algiers:
To his harem assembled: 'My dears,
   You may think it odd of me,
   But I've given up sodomy.
Tonight's for you girls.' (*Loud cheers*)

ANON.

There was a young man named Racine
Who invented a fucking machine:
   Concave and convex,
   It would fit either sex,
With attractions for those in between.

ANON.

There was a young woman of Dee,
Who stayed with each man she did see;
   When it came to the rest,
   She wished to be best,
And practice makes perfect, you see.

ANON.

There once was a Fellow of Wadham,
Who approved of the doings of Sodom;
   For a man might, he said,
   Have a very poor head,
But be a good fellow at bottom.

ANON.

There was a young Fellow of Wadham,
Who asked for a ticket to Sodom;
   When they said: 'We prefer
   Not to issue them, Sir.'
He said: 'Don't call me "Sir"! Call me "Modom".'

ANON.

There was a young lady of Ealing,
And her lover before her was kneeling;
   She said: 'Dearest Jim,
   Take your hand from my quim –
I much prefer fucking to feeling.'

                  ISAAC ASIMOV

There was a young lady of Exeter,
So pretty that men craned their necks at her;
   One was even so brave
   As to take out and wave
The distinguishing marks of his sex at her.

                  ANON.

A lonely young fellow of Eton
Used always to sleep with the heat on,
   Till he met a young lass,
   Who showed him her ass –
Now they're sleeping with only a sheet on.

                  ANON.

A pansy who lived in Khartoum
Took a lesbian up to his room;
   And they argued all night
   As to who had the right
To do what and with which and to whom.

                  ANON.

There once was a judge of Assize
Whose bollocks were not the same size;
    He'd look at the right
    With a gasp of delight,
But the left one brought tears to his eyes.

ANON.

A yogi from far-off Beirut
For women did not care a hoot,
    But his organ would stand
    In a manner quite grand,
When a snake-charmer played on his flute.

ANON.

A mechanical marvel was Bill,
He'd a tool that was shaped like a quill;
    With this fabulous dink,
    He could squirt purple ink,
And decorate lampshades at will.

ANON.

There was an old fellow of Fife,
Who lived a lascivious life;
    When his organ was limp
    Like an over-boned shrimp,
He brought what was left to his wife.

ANON.

FOR WIDOWER – wanted, house-keeper,
Not too bloody refined, a light sleeper;
   When employer's inclined,
   Must be game for a grind,
Pay generous, mind, but can't keep her.

ANON.

Shed a tear for the WREN named McGinnis,
Who brought her career to a finis;
   She did not understand
   The sudden command
To break out the Admiral's pinnace.

ANON.

There was a young bride named McWing,
Who thought sex a delirious fling.
   When her bridegroom grew ill
   From too much (as they will),
She found other men do the same thing.

ANON.

An innocent bride from the Mission,
Remarked, on her first night's coition:
   'What an intimate section
   To use for connection,
And, lord! what a silly position!'

ANON.

A rapist, who reeked of cheap booze,
Attempted to ravish Miss Hughes;
   She cried: 'I suppose
   There's no time for my clothes,
But PLEASE let me take off my shoes!'
ANON.

There was a young lady of Brabant,
Who slept with an impotent savant.
   She admitted: 'We shouldn't,
   But it turned out he couldn't,
So you can't say we have, when we haven't.'
ANON.

[*Maud Fitzgerald*]

A delighted, incredulous bride,
Remarked to her groom at her side:
   'I never could quite
   Believe till tonight
Our anatomies *would* coincide.'
ANON.

To his bride said a numbskull named Clarence:
'I trust you will show some forbearance.
   My sexual habits
   I picked up from rabbits,
And occasionally watching my parents.'
ANON.

There was a young fellow called Chubb
Who joined a smart buggery club;
    But his parts were so small,
    He was no use at all,
And they promptly refunded his sub.

ANON.

King Louis gave lessons in Class.
One day, when he lay with a lass,
    When she used the word 'Damn',
    He said to her: 'Ma'am,
Keep a more civil tongue in my ass.'

ANON.

There was a young man of Ghent,
Whose tool was so long, that it bent;
    To save himself trouble,
    He put it in double,
And instead of coming, he went.

ANON.

A young lady, whose life-style the malicious
Described loosely, as too meretricious,
    Said: 'When the boys peel me
    And delightfully feel me,
I feel like a Golden Delicious.'

GAVIN EWART

There was a young girl of Darjeeling,
Who danced with such exquisite feeling;
    There was never a sound
    For miles around,
Save of fly-buttons hitting the ceiling.

                        ANON.

A policeman from Nottingham Junction,
Whose organs had long ceased to function,
    Deceived his good wife
    For the rest of her life
With the aid of his constable's truncheon.

                        ANON.

A lass of curvacious physique
Liked dresses that made her look *chic*,
    But all could agree
    That topless to knee
Did little to help her *mystique*.

                DOUGLAS CATLEY

There was a young man of Dumfries,
Who said to his girl: 'If you please,
    It would give me great bliss,
    If, while playing with this,
You could give some attention to these.'

                        ANON.

There was a young lady of Lundy,
Began fresh affairs every Monday;
    Thus enlarging each week,
    Her erotic technique,
Whilst chastely abstaining each Sunday.

W.F.N.WATSON

There was a young plumber of Leigh,
Who was plumbing his girl by the sea
    She said: 'Stop your plumbing!
    There's somebody coming!'
Said the plumber, still plumbing: 'It's me.'

ANON.

Well-buggered was a boy named Depasse
By all of the lads in his class;
    He said, with a yawn:
    'When the novelty's gone,
It's only a pain in the ass.'

ANON.

There was a young lady called Hilda,
Who went for a walk with a builder;
    He knew that he could,
    And he should and he would,
And he did, and it bloody near killed her.

ANON.

A bashful young fellow of Brighton
Would never make love with the light on;
   His girl-friend said: 'Noel!
   You're in the wrong hole.
There's plenty of room in the right 'un.'

E. O. PARROTT

A lady of features cherubic
Was famed for her area pubic;
   When they asked its size,
   She said with surprise:
'Are you speaking of square feet, or cubic?'

ANON.

A couple there was in Blefuscu,
Making love in a night of subfusc hue,
   But some headlights drew near,
   And made it quite clear
They were right at the head of a bus queue.

W.F.N.WATSON

There was a young fellow called Price,
Who dabbled in all sorts of vice;
   He had virgins and boys,
   And mechanical toys,
And on Mondays he meddled with mice.

ANON.

There was a young fellow called Shit,
A name he disliked quite a bit;
   So he changed it to Shite –
   A step in the right
Direction, one has to admit.

VICTOR GRAY

A much-worried mother once said:
'My dear, you've been kissing young Fred
   Since six, it's now ten;
   Do it just once again,
And then start thinking of bed.'

ANON.

There was a young lady called Smith
Whose virtue was mostly a myth;
   She said: 'Try as I can,
   I can't find a man
That it's fun to be virtuous with.'

ANON.

There was a young girl of Mauritius,
Who said: 'No, I'm not really vicious.
   I get no sexual kick
   Out of sucking this prick.
It's just that it tastes so delicious.'

VICTOR GRAY

There was a young lawyer called Rex,
Who was sadly deficient in sex;
   Arraigned for exposure,
   He said, with composure:
'*De minimus, non curat lex.*'

ANON.

There was a young lady of Rye
With a shape like a capital 'I';
   When they told her she had,
   She learned how to pad,
Which shows you that figures can lie.

ANON.

A young man with passions quite gingery,
Tore a hole in his sister's lingerie;
   He slapped her behind
   And made up his mind
To add incest to insult and injury.

ANON.

A prostitute living in London,
Went pantless, with zippers all undone;
   She'd explain: 'Well, you see
   I can do two or three,
While Ruby next door's getting one done.'

DOUGLAS CATLEY

There was a young fellow called Bliss,
Whose sex-life was sadly amiss.
   For even with Venus,
   His recalcitrant penis
Would never do better than T
                 H
                 I
                 S

ANON.

Thus spake an old Chinese mandarin:
'There's a subject I'd like to use candour in.
   The geese of Pekin
   Are so steeped in sin
They'd as soon let a man as a gander in.'

ANON.

A plumber from Lowater Creek
Was called to a girl with a leak;
   She looked so becoming,
   That he fixed all her plumbing
And didn't emerge for a week.

ANON.

[On Board Starship *Enterprise*]

Though most of the crewmen are whites,
Uhura has full equal rights.
   Her crew-mates, you see,
   Love De-mo-cra-cy,
And the way that she fills out her tights.

ANON.

Meanwhile, back home at the ranch,
I was fucking a cowgirl called Blanche;
  She said: 'It's a change
  From riding the range,
But I still prefer brandy-and-branch.'

VICTOR GRAY

A certain young sheik I'm not namin',
Asked a flapper he thought he was tamin':
  'Have you your maidenhead?'
  'Don't be silly!' she said,
'But I still have the box that it came in.'

ANON.

The first chap to fuck little Sophie
Was awarded the Kraft-Ebing Trophy;
  Thus ten thousand quid
  For what the chap did
Will be widely considered a low fee.

VICTOR GRAY

There was a young lady called Etta,
Who fancied herself in a sweater;
  Three reasons she had:
  Keeping warm was not bad,
But the other two reasons were better.

ANON.

A shiftless young fellow of Kent,
Had his wife fuck the landlord for rent;
    But as she grew older,
    The landlord grew colder,
And now they live out in a tent.

ANON.

There was a young lady called Flynn,
Who thought fornication a sin;
    But when she was tight,
    She thought it all right,
So everyone filled her with gin.

ANON.

There was a young girl of Cape Cod,
Who thought babies were fashioned by God,
    But 'twas not the Almighty
    Who lifted her nightie,
But Roger the lodger, the sod.

ANON.

'It's my custom,' said dear Lady Norris,
'To hitch lifts from the drivers of lorries.
    I see when they pee
    Details hidden from me
At the wheel of my second-hand Morris.'

ANON.

A 'brickie' who had a fine tool,
Was thought by his girl-friend too cool,
    Since, when he was up her,
    He broke for a cupper,
As that was his union rule.

E. O. PARROTT

There was a young faggot called Willy,
Whose antics were now and then silly;
    He once had, for fun,
    A vasectomy done –
A clear case of 'gelding the lily'.

KENNETH PETCHENIK

At the orgy I humped twenty-two,
And was glad when the whole thing was through;
    I don't find it swinging
    To do all this change-ringing,
But at orgies, what else can you do?

ANON.

There was a young fellow named Menzies,
Whose kissing sent girls into frenzies,
    But a virgin one night
    Crossed her legs in a fright,
And fractured his bi-focal lenses.

ANON.

There was an old man of Lugano,
Who constructed a bog of Meccano,
  Which sharpened his wits
  And aided his shits –
Mens sana in corpore sano.

VICTOR GRAY

There was a young girl of La Plata,
Who was widely renowned as a farter;
  Her deafening reports
  At the Argentine Sports
Made her much in demand as a starter.

ANON.

Sir John Shagbag (Conservative, Nore):
'The Honourable Lady's a whore.
  Even now, you know what:
  Churchill's prick's in her twat.'
(Some applause. Labour cries of 'Withdraw')

VICTOR GRAY

Said a gloomy young fellow called Fart:
'This name's bad enough for a start.
  But my snob of a Dad
  Makes it twice as bad
With his ruddy Sir Mark Ffart-ffart, Bart.'

VICTOR GRAY

Envoi

'*Scorn not the sonnet, critic. . .*'

Then scorn not the limerick either,
Though as Tennyson said, who knows why the
  Fuck such a rhyme
  Makes the grim reaper Time
Such a markedly blither old scyther.

ROBERT CONQUEST

ACKNOWLEDGEMENTS

My grateful thanks are due to the following, who have supplied me with material and information or who have otherwise helped with the compilation of this book: Isaac Asimov, Gaby Astinax, Jonathan Barker of the Arts Council Poetry Library, Adrian Benjamin, D. H. Clibborn, Robert Conquest, John H. Coxall, Ivan Cresswell, Francis Davis, Jennie Davis of Michael Joseph Ltd, Gavin Ewart, Martin Fagg, William Harmon of Oxford University Press, Mrs D. Higham, H. Russell Jones, O.B.E., Peter Jones of the *New Statesman*, Gershon Legman, Frances Mackenzie, O.B.E., E. Maidanik, Arthur Marshall, S. Nowell-Smith, Bernard Palmer of the *Church Times*, Tricia Parrott, William Parrott, J.P., Mike Rees, Charles Seaton of the *Spectator*, Anne Serrailler, Ida Thurtle and Lady Worlledge.

I should also like to thank the following for permission to reproduce limericks or other material in this volume: The Bodley Head Ltd, for a limerick by C. E. M. Joad; Jonathan Cape Ltd, for a limerick from *The Poetry of Robert Frost*, this limerick also reprinted by permission of Holt, Rinehart & Winston from *Robert Frost: Poetry and Prose*, edited by Edward Connery Latham and Lawrance Thompson, copyright © 1972 by Holt, Rinehart & Winston; Curtis Brown, London, and Curtis Brown Associates Ltd, New York, on behalf of the Estate of Ogden Nash, for sixteen limericks and four limicks by Ogden Nash; Faber & Faber Ltd, for 'T. S. Eliot is quite at a loss' from *Academic Graffiti*, 'The Marquis de Sade and Genet' from *Marginalia*, and 'As the poets have mournfully sung' from *Shorts*, all from *Collected Poems* by W. H. Auden; Granada Publishing Ltd and Laura A. Huxley, for various limericks from *The Lure of the Limerick* by W. Baring-Gould; David Higham Associates Ltd and Harold Ober Associates, for 'The last time I slept with the Queen' by Dylan Thomas from *The Silver Treasury of Light Verse*, published by The American Library, New York; Hutchinson Books Ltd and Simon & Schuster Inc., for 'A Man from the Washington Post' from *Earthly Powers* by Anthony Burgess, copyright © 1980 by Anthony Burgess; Michael Joseph Ltd, for limericks from *The Best and Only 101 Limericks of Spike Milligan* by Spike Milligan, published by Michael Joseph Ltd with M. & J. Hobbs; Kryptádia Inc., for 109 limericks from *The Limerick* published by Jupiter Books, London, and *The New Limerick*, published by Crown Publishers Inc., New York, both edited by Gershon Legman; Macmillan Publishing Co. Inc., New York, for limericks from *An Explosion of Limericks* (1967), edited by Vyvyan Holland, and *Out on a Limerick* (1960), edited by Bennet

Cerf; Methuen & Co. Ltd, for a limerick by Rev. W. R. Inge from *The Everyman Century of Humorous Verse*, published by J. M. Dent & Sons Ltd; John Murray (Publishers) Ltd, for 'Summer' from *The Best of Betjeman* by Sir John Betjeman; Oxford University Press, for limericks from *The Oxford Book of Light Verse* (1938), edited by W. H. Auden, *The New Oxford Book of Light Verse* (1978), edited by Kingsley Amis, and *The Oxford Book of American Light Verse*, edited by W. Harmon; Penguin Books Ltd, for limericks from *Yet More Comic and Curious Verse*, edited by J. M. Cohen; G. P. Putnam's Sons, New York, for nine limericks from *Spilt Milk* by Morris Bishop, copyright © 1942 by Morris Bishop, renewed 1969; the *Church Times*, the *New Statesman* and the *Spectator*, for limericks taken from their literary competitions; *Punch*, for various limericks including 'A Scientist living in Staines' by R. J. P. Hewison; the organizers of the Cheltenham Festival, for various limericks; Stone's Ginger Wine, for a limerick by A. B. Hall.

I am also indebted to the Estate of Conrad Aiken, for nine limericks by Conrad Aiken from *Limericks* copyright © Conrad Aiken, 1963, 1964, reprinted by permission of Brandt and Brandt Literary Agents Inc., and from *A Seizure of Limericks* copyright © Conrad Aiken, 1963, 1964, reprinted by permission of Brandt and Brandt Literary Agents Inc. and published by W. H. Allen & Co. Ltd (1965); Isaac Asimov, for his limericks from *Lecherous Limericks*, published by Panther Books Ltd; Cyril Bibby, for limericks and a prose extract from his book *The Art of the Limerick* published by the Research Publishing Co.; Tony Butler, for a limerick from *Best Irish Limericks* (1970), edited by himself and published by Wolfe Publishing; Mrs Douglas Catley of Cape Catley Ltd, for limericks from *A Dabble of Limericks* by the late Douglas Catley; the Literary Trustees of Walter de la Mare and the Society of Authors as their representative, for 'Buttons' from *The Collected Works of Walter de la Mare*; The Society of Authors as the literary representative of the Estate of James Joyce, for a limerick by James Joyce; Jean Harrowven, for eleven limericks from her book *The Limerick Makers*, published by the Research Publishing Co., and also for the text extract from this book; Sir Rupert Hart-Davis, for a limerick by William Plomer; Mrs Laura Huxley and Chatto & Windus Ltd, for a limerick by Aldous Huxley from *The Lure of the Limerick* by W. Baring-Gould; Joyce Johnson, for limericks by herself and Leslie Johnson; Cyril Ray, for limericks from his book *Lickerish Limericks*, published by J. M. Dent & Sons Ltd; Langford Reed, for various limericks (see separate note below); Louise H. Sclove, for 'Hereditary' by Arthur Guiterman.

Last, but not least, I am grateful to the following for permission to include limericks in this volume: Paul Alexander, Peter Alexander, Jim Anthony, Gerard Benson, Gina Berkeley, A. Cinna, Alan Clark, Robert Conquest, Wendy Cope, Coral E. Copping. A. P. Cox, C. D. Cudmore, Frank

Davies, Gavin Ewart, Margaret Galbreath, Richard Leighton Greene, Bill Greenwell, Paul Griffin, Gerry Hamill, Gordon Harper, Mark Holtby, Tim Hopkins, Prebendary Philip Husbands, J. H. Lee, T. L. McCarthy, Frank McManus, George McWilliam, Harriet Mandelbaum, I. D. M. Morley, Betty Morris, Cyril Mountjoy, Veronica Nicolson, Violet Ormerod, Kenneth Petchenik, Fiona Pitt-Kethley, Pascoe Polglaze, A. G. Prys-Jones, Moss Rich, Frank Richards, J. M. Ross, Ron Rubin, Stanley J. Sharpless, Ruth Silcock, Sidney Bernard Smith, John Stanley, Andrew Stoker, Kirkham Talbot, Richard Taylor, Harry Thomas, R. K. R. Thornton, Ida Thurtle, Claudio Vita-Finzi, Lt. Col. W. F. N. Watson, David Woodsford and Reg Yearley.

The publisher gratefully acknowledges Little, Brown and Co. for permission to include the following limericks: 'There was a young lady named Harris' and 'There was an old gossip called Baird' from *Primrose Path* copyright 1935 by Ogden Nash; 'Benjamin Arthur Carlotta' and 'Requiem' from *The Face is Familiar* by Ogden Nash copyright 1938, 1940 by Ogden Nash; 'First Limick', 'Second Limick', 'Third Limick' and 'Fifth Limick' from *Versus* by Ogden Nash copyright 1948 by the Curtis Publishing Company; 'Limerick Three' from *The Private Dining Room* by Ogden Nash copyright 1951 by Ogden Nash; 'A lama of Outer Mongolia', 'An old Danish jester named Yorick', 'A novelist of the absurd' and 'A crusader's wife shipped from the garrison' copyright © 1965, 1967 by Ogden Nash.

Every effort has been made to trace copyright holders. We would be grateful to hear from any copyright holders not here acknowledged.

INDEX